Give Attention to Reading

Through the New Testament in Six Months

compiled by

Edwin Crozier

ISBN 0-9777829-1-3

Cover Design by James Wood

To order additional copies:

www.streamsidesupplies.com
Call (877) 644-3225
Write to Streamside Supplies; 95 Oak Valley Dr. Spring Hill, TN, 37174;

Printed in the United States of America

"Give Attention to Reading"

Reading the
New Testament in Six Months

Daily Bible Study

Introduction

As I prepared this material, I wanted to start off with a great story or illustration to emphasize how daily Bible reading would help you. Where would I come up with such a story? Never fear. I would Google it.

I Googled "bible reading stories illustrations." I was certain I would uncover a story to stop you in your tracks and drive into your heart the need to read your Bible. Was I amazed?

The first three pages of entries had to do with children's Bible books or how to read Bible stories to kids. It reminded me of a song I heard a few years back.

Following the tragic attack of 9-11, Alan Jackson released a song entitled "*Where Were You (When the World Stopped Turning)*". The last half of the chorus says, "But I know Jesus and I talk to God / And I remember this from when I was young / Faith, hope and love are some good things He gave us / and the greatest is love."

Why did he have to go back to when he was young to remember **I Corinthians 13:13** says, "But now faith, hope, love, abide these three; but the greatest of these is love"?

Regrettably, too many people view the Bible as a children's story book. We need to view it as a constant life companion and guide for all ages. In **II Timothy 3:14-15**, Paul told Timothy, "You, however, continue in the things you have learned and become convinced of, knowing from whom you have learned them, and that from childhood you have known the sacred writings which are able to give you the wisdom that leads to salvation through faith which is in Christ Jesus" (**NASU**). Certainly, Bible knowledge should begin in childhood, but it must be continued through adulthood and never forgotten.

In **I Timothy 4:13**, Paul encouraged Timothy, "Till I come, give attention to reading..." (**NKJV**). We must give attention to reading God's word—publicly and privately. That is what this book is all about.

We need to give attention to reading. Why? Is it because that is God's homework assignment for His disciples? Absolutely not. We must give attention to reading because we are at war. "Our struggle is not against flesh and blood, but against the rulers, against the powers, against the world forces of this darkness, against the spiritual forces of wickedness in the heavenly places. Therefore, take up the full armor of God" (**Ephesians 6:12-13**).

Look at that enemy again. Do you think we can beat that enemy? Of course not. We are only human. God, however, can beat our enemy. Therefore, we must put on God's armor. Like David who walked onto the battlefield to face Goliath, we do not wear the armor provided by men, but by God. From where does that armor come? The Word of God. Each piece of armor in **Ephesians 6:14-17** comes directly from the

Word. **John 17:17** said God's word is the truth with which our loins will be girt. Our heart can be protected with righteousness in which we are trained by scriptures according to **II Timothy 3:16-17**. Our feet are shod with the gospel, which according to **Colossians 1:5** is the word of truth. Our shield of faith comes by hearing and hearing by the word of God according to **Romans 10:17**. The salvation which protects our head comes from God's word according to **Acts 20:32** and **II Timothy 3:15**.

This study is designed to help you suit up in God's armor every day. This will help you develop a daily habit of Bible reading, arming you to face Satan on the battlefield of life.

Certainly there are times when we need to open our Bibles, get out the dictionaries and commentaries and pour over the intricate details of the Scripture's meaning. Yet, more fundamentally, we simply need to make the Bible a part of our lives. We do this through continued, habitual reading. You will be amazed at how your view of our world and your place in it will change simply by reading God's word every day.

Every aspect of this book is designed to promote this one issue—daily, continued habitual Bible reading. If you work all the way through this book on schedule, you will read the entire New Testament in six months. To accomplish this, you will read two chapters per day, five days per week. Why five days? Why not seven? Because it is designed to help you develop a habit, not overwhelm you. I trust that on Sunday's you are meeting with a local congregation to read and study God's Word. Why not six? Because I recognize life happens. If you accomplish all five of your readings on schedule, use day six to read something from the Old Testament or to get ahead. If not, day six can be a day to catch up.

You can easily see this material is designed to be used in a small group setting. The reason for this is elementary. We follow through on developing habits better when we have to meet with other people to discuss how we did. They hold us accountable. If you are not working through this book with a small group, at least establish a relationship with another Christian or family to hold one another accountable.

With each reading, I have provided five simple questions. These are not "five questions to show what is most important in the chapters." They are basic questions to help you focus on the reading and overcome the tendency to skim. How many times have you read through a chapter only to realize your mind wandered after the fifth verse? We pay more attention to our reading when we are searching for answers.

There are also four thought questions with each day's reading, these are provided to help you make this study as deep as you want and need it to be. I have included a lesson on *"Life-Changing Bible Study"* following this introduction to help you understand the basis for those four questions.

At the end of each week's readings, I have provided a page of group discussion questions. Even if you are working through this material alone, I encourage you to consider and answer the questions on that page. One of the greatest helps to learning anything is repetition. Working through the group discussion page is a great way to remember some of the more important lessons you uncovered in your daily readings.

If you are working through this with a small group, I want to stress that the purpose of this material is to help you develop a positive habit of Bible reading. It is not designed to be a weekly study of "Edwin's five favorite lessons" from each week's reading. Therefore, please, do not feel pressured to work through all nine questions each week in the group discussion. The first four questions about what each reader learned, questioned or struggled with are far more important than the questions I provided to help prompt group discussion on specific issues if necessary. I would far rather you spend your time as a group helping other Christians answer their questions or having other Christians help you answer yours, than making sure you answer all of mine.

Additionally, I have used the New American Standard 1995 Updated Edition as I prepared this material. Though I have tried to keep the questions as generic as possible, if at anytime you struggle with a question, you may want to check the NASU translation to see if that helps the question make more sense.

Finally, if you are using this material in a group setting and you have children in your home, let me encourage you to keep your children involved. Do the daily readings as a family. Allow the children to be involved in the group discussions as well. Our children need to hear adults discuss God's word. Of course, they will not understand everything. But they will understand Bible reading and discussion are important. Beyond that, you may be surprised what your children pick up.

As you work through this book, you will not read directly from **Matthew** to **Revelation**. Rather, the readings are loosely arranged in author and thematic groups. We will read Luke's books together, John's books together, Peter's books together (along with Mark's gospel, which is connected to Peter and Jude's letter that is similar to Peter's). To help spread the gospels out more evenly, Paul's epistles are interspersed throughout the readings.

Below is the order in which you will read:

1. Luke
2. Acts
3. Romans
4. Galatians
5. Ephesians
6. Philippians
7. Colossians
8. Mark
9. I Peter
10. II Peter
11. Jude
12. I Corinthians
13. II Corinthians
14. I Thessalonians
15. II Thessalonians
16. Matthew
17. Hebrews
18. James
19. Philemon
20. I Timothy
21. II Timothy
22. Titus
23. John
24. I John
25. II John
26. III John
27. Revelation

By the time you are done with this material, you should have a firmly developed habit of Bible reading. Do not stop just because you have finished this book. Rather, keep up your habit. Read through the New Testament again using a different translation or a different order. Or start reading the Old Testament. Whatever approach you take, keep your reading up.

May God richly bless you as you draw closer to Him through daily reading of His Word. More importantly, may you richly bless God.

Reading Your Bible

Along with each daily assignment, there are four thought questions to help you apply what you are reading. These questions can help you make the study as deep as you want to make it.

The four questions are based on **II Timothy 3:16-17**. In that passage, Paul explained that the Scriptures are profitable because they accomplish four necessary actions in order to make us complete.

To help you understand these questions, I have included a sermon outline that explains how to have life-changing Bible study.

Please, read through the following sermon to help prepare you for the assignments of this book.

How Do You Read Your Bible?
Life-Changing Bible Study

Introduction:

When you examine the disciples described in the New Testament, what kind of people do you find? Jesus had disciples like Peter, James and John—stalwart in the faith. But He also had Judas—a hypocrite and a thief. The Jerusalem church had members like Stephen and Barnabas—faithful and generous to the end. But it also had members like Ananias and Sapphira. Paul had men travel with him like Timothy and Titus—strong teachers who taught others. But he also had Demas—who forsook him for this present world. It is no wonder that Paul, in **II Timothy 2:20-21**, wrote of a large house with some vessels for honor and some for dishonor. The vessels for honor are men and women who lead changed lives, while the vessels of dishonor revert back to worldly ways. The honorable vessels are cleansing themselves, becoming "prepared for every good work." But they do not do this alone. According to **II Timothy 3:15-17**, God provided the Scripture so we can be vessels of honor, equipped and prepared for every good work. Because of the Bible, we lead changed lives and continue to change our lives, growing to become more and more like Christ. Regrettably, however, many of us get to the point that we think, "Sure, I have a problem here or there, but overall, I am pretty good." With that mindset, the Bible becomes useless as a life-changing tool. We begin to read the Bible differently. In many cases, it ceases to be a guide and simply becomes a reference book. When that happens, we no longer grow. If we quit growing, we are no longer ensured salvation (**II Peter 1:5-11**). Therefore, we must ask ourselves, "How do we read the Bible?" Examine some common methods of Bible study and how they fall short of changing our lives. Then examine the Bible model for life-changing Bible study. Finally, examine yourself. How do you read your Bible?

Discussion:

I. *Common Bible study methods that will not change your life.* In the following list are methods that should never be used, methods that are proper for certain goals but not for changing your life and methods that are a good start but do not go far enough.

    A. <u>The Procrastination Method</u>: We can be masters at putting off Bible study. Too many people plan to study their Bibles, but never get around to it. In the end, they rarely study. This method should never be followed. Good intentions will never change your life.

    B. <u>The Study by Proxy Method</u>: Some people only "study" their Bible's on Sunday, when they listen to a preacher. This is study by proxy, because the listener is not studying at all. Rather, he is allowing someone else's study to substitute for his own. This method should never be used. Do not get me wrong, sermons should be listened to carefully. You may learn a lot from a sermon. But listening to a sermon is not intended to be your Bible study. Rather, it is intended to be a jumping off place for your own study (**Acts 17:11**).

    C. <u>The Bible Class Preparation Method</u>: Perhaps some Bible class lessons are so difficult, challenging and thought provoking that when you have prepared for them you have performed some life-changing study. Typically, however, preparing for class is no more than answering simple questions and writing down what you already knew. Everyone should prepare for every class. But rarely will this change your life.

D. <u>The Debate Method</u>: This is studying to prove a point. No doubt, there are times when we must study so we can improve our defense of the truth. However, this method will rarely change our lives because it is not intended to change our lives, but someone else's. Keep in mind that many people who have become masters at proving their point have fallen into sin. Their study did not change their lives.

E. <u>The Studying to Teach Method</u>: Most of us know we learn more when we are teaching a class. We may, therefore, think that studying so we can teach is the study method that changes our lives. While it is a good start, by itself this study will not change our lives. Studying to teach others is still focused on others. Its purpose is to give information to others, not change our lives. Allow me to illustrate. I spent my last year and a half of college in Florence, AL, working with Harold Comer and David Thomley at the College View church in a training program. Around the time of my graduation, David and I went out for a cup of coffee and some conversation. David asked me two questions that stunned me and impacted my thinking forever. He first asked me if I thought I was a better preacher than when I had moved to Florence. "Of course," I answered. I knew more and I was better at presenting it. His second questioned floored me. "Are you a better Christian?" I learned that day that I can know more Bible and be better able to communicate it, but still not be a better Christian. Changing our lives is not about teaching others. It is about applying our knowledge to our lives.

F. <u>The Devotional Method</u>, also known as the <u>Read Through the Bible in a Year Method</u>: Most people who study their Bibles at all, use this method. In this method, the student spends a little time every day reading a passage from the Bible and then praying. Allow me to say, I think every Christian should do this. However, devotional study by itself will not change our lives. Why? Because devotional style reading is more emotionally based. These types of study are designed to make people feel good, so they can face the day strengthened and encouraged. That is wonderful and necessary. But to change our lives, typically we have to feel bad. In fact, Jesus put it this way in the Sermon on the Mount, "Blessed are those who mourn, for they shall be comforted" (**Matthew 5:4**). We do not make changes when we feel good about the way we live. We make changes when we feel sorrow.

G. Are these your methods of study? If so, can I challenge you to dig deeper with your Bible? Some of these methods are great starts, but are not life-changing. In order to change your life, you must first make sure to approach your Bible and your life with the proper attitude. Then you must conduct your study with personal change in mind. **II Timothy 3:15-16** instructs us regarding both of these aspects of study.

II. The attitudes with which I must approach the Bible (**II Timothy 3:15-16**).
A. The Bible is sacred (**II Timothy 3:15**).
1. I understand that the paper and binding of the book is not holy. There are no rules about cleanliness and touching a Bible. I remember once when I was placing my Bible under the pew in front of me so I could retrieve it easily, my grandfather said, "I never put my Bible on the floor." "Why not," I innocently asked. "Because," he replied, "that is where people's feet have been." "Oh," I responded, "Where do you put your Bible?" "Next to me on the pew," he said. "What part of their body has been there?" I asked. We are not to teach "bibliolatry", that is, the worship of this book. Thus there are no rules about how to handle the book itself. But when we open our Bibles to drink in what we find inside, we are walking on holy ground.
2. The scriptures are sacred and holy. The messages contained therein are not to be taken lightly. We are to revere what we read in the Bible. As Moses was afraid and trembled at the burning bush (**Exodus 3:6**), accordingly we should tremble and be afraid as we read the scriptures. Though it contains many stories, the Bible is not a novel to be read for entertainment. Though it contains much teaching, it is not a textbook to be read dryly and without life. Though it contains much history, it is not a reference book about dead people and distant events. This book contains Jesus' words of life (**cf. John 6:68**). As such, it is the most important book on the face of the earth. Every time we open it we should handle it with care, approach it with caution and expect to be changed by its sacred message.

B. The Bible will give me wisdom that leads to salvation (**II Timothy 3:15**).
   1. I do not have the wisdom that leads to salvation. I have to get it from the sacred message of the Bible. When we have been Christians for a while, we sometimes want to tell the folks in the denominations that they do not have the wisdom that leads to salvation. They need to read their Bible's better. We think we have already accomplished this task. But notice to whom Paul is speaking. He is speaking to Timothy, a man who had been reading and learning the scriptures from his childhood. He was a preacher of the gospel. Yet Paul reminded him to get wisdom from scripture. He did not already possess all of it.
   2. If I ever believe I have all the wisdom that leads to salvation, I will approach the Bible with a different attitude. I will no longer be able to change when necessary. I will quit growing. If I quit growing, I have died. Thus, I must always approach the Bible with the attitude that I am supposed to get something out of it. Getting this wisdom will lead me to salvation.
C. The Bible is inspired by God (**II Timothy 3:16**).
   1. I must approach the Bible understanding from Whom it has come. Though God worked through man, the Bible is not a man made book. The words contained in this book did not come by an act of human will. Rather, men moved by the Holy Spirit spoke from God (**II Peter 1:21**). I must read it accordingly. When men write a book, I can take it or leave it. I can take from it what I want and leave the rest behind to rot. When men write something I can often allow their writings to mean what I want them to mean. When I approach the Bible, I cannot do this. God has written this book and I am not allowed to add to it or take away from it. God has written this book and I must get from it what God wanted me to get. I cannot change the message in any way. If I do so, it is to my own destruction (**II Peter 3:16**).
   2. We have all heard the popular saying, "God gave the 10 commandments, not the 10 suggestions." We chuckle, but this statement encapsulates the way we must approach all scripture. What we read is not good advice. It is not nice things we should do, but do not really have to. This is God's word to us for how we are to conduct our lives. When we approach it, we must be quick to hear and apply it and slow to speak and get angry with it (**James 1:19**). When I open my Bible, I must prepare to be told how to live by the One who has the authority to tell me. I must accept what He commands and change my life.

III. Four questions that will change my life when I study my Bible (**II Timothy 3:16**).
   A. <u>Teaching</u>: *What do I learn from this study?*
      1. This is the most basic question we will ask. It has to do with information and facts. To answer this question we will use different study aids: dictionaries, lexicons, commentaries, etc. We will solicit others for help. At all times, we must study in the Biblical context, never missing the forest because of the trees. We should never get so caught up in studying a character, a word, a verse or a chapter that we take it out of its place in the Bible. Whatever information we find must coincide with everything else the Bible says.
      2. Some of the methods we described earlier will take us this far. The "Studying to Teach Method" will help us answer this first question far better than any other approach. But, please, keep in mind, when you have accomplished this much study you have only asked one of the four questions. You have only gone 25% of the way to a changed life. Never be satisfied with simply knowing more about the Bible.
   B. <u>Reproof</u>: *Where do I fall short according to this study?*
      1. To reprove someone means to convict or convince them regarding sin in their lives (**Luke 3:19; Ephesians 5:11; et al**). **Romans 3:23** claims we have all fallen short of God's glory. It stands to reason then, that when I approach the Bible it should strike me somewhere.
      2. When I open my Bible, I must recognize that I am going to find out something that is wrong in my life. I hope that is not seen as negative. I know we like to be told all the good things we are doing. There will be lots of study that shows us what we are doing right. But if I am going to change, I must find out what I am doing wrong.
   C. <u>Correction</u>: *What must I change according to this study?*
      1. The term "correction" in **II Timothy 3:16** refers to restoring a fallen object to its upright position. When we answered the last question, we learned there are some things toppled over in

our lives. Answering this question allows us to determine what changes to implement to set things up right again. We have now gone from determining what is wrong, to determining how to fix it.

    2.   We must ask several subordinate questions: "What must I stop doing according to this study?" "What must I start doing according to this study?" "What must I improve and grow in according to this study?" Without answering these questions, our lives will never be changed. If you make it this far in studying your Bible, you are close to a changed life.

D. <u>Training in righteousness</u>: *What habits must I develop according to this study?*

    1.   Training focuses us on discipline and habit. Righteousness has to do with living a right life before God. Scripture helps us form habits that discipline us to be right with God.

    2.   There are things that are toppled over in our lives. We have determined what must be corrected to set those things aright. Now, we apply our earlier answers to our lives. We turn from inward examination to outward application. Answering this question changes our lives because we answer this question, not with words, but with actions. We answer this question, not on paper, but in daily activity. At this point, we may use the "Devotional Method" of Bible study to encourage us in our daily actions, strengthening us to face the day and do what we know we must even when it does not come naturally.

Conclusion:

How do you read your Bible? Is it a book that sits waiting for a convenient time to be opened? Is it a book you simply take with you to Bible class and worship? Is it a reference book to be searched when you are trying to prove a point or simply wanting to learn how to teach? Or is it a book that changes your life daily, drawing you closer to the Master, making you more useful in His kingdom and more equipped for every good work (**II Timothy 2:21; 3:17**)?

Change does not come easy for us. We like our comfort zones. But we can change. You can break free from the chains of spiritual mediocrity with which Satan would like to bind you. Approach the Scripture with the intent to be changed. Before figuring out what to teach others, see where you need to be changed and let your study change you.

Week 1; Day 1—Date _____
Luke 1-2

(In the space below, write any notes or thoughts you have regarding the text you are reading today.)

Thought Questions:
1. Write briefly what you have learned from this chapter?

2. Where do you fall short according to this chapter?

3. What do you need to change according to this chapter?

Questions regarding today's reading:

1. To whom in particular did Luke write this gospel?

2. Who were the two women who became miraculously pregnant?

3. What did Zacharias name his son? Why?

4. What habits do you need to develop according to this chapter?

4. Who visited Jesus while He was still in the manger?

5. Who were the man and woman who blessed God when they saw Jesus in Jerusalem?

Week 1; Day 2—Date _____
Luke 3-4
(In the space below, write any notes or thoughts you have regarding the text you are reading today.)

Questions regarding today's reading:

1. Who was Caesar when John the Baptist was preaching?

2. What kind of fruits did John say those who would be baptized by him had to bring forth?

3. What happened when John baptized Jesus?

4. List the three temptations of Jesus?

5. Whose mother-in-law did Jesus heal?

Thought Questions:

1. Write briefly what you have learned from this chapter?

2. Where do you fall short according to this chapter?

3. What do you need to change according to this chapter?

4. What habits do you need to develop according to this chapter?

Week 1; Day 3—Date _____
Luke 5-6

(In the space below, write any notes or thoughts you have regarding the text you are reading today.)

1. Write briefly what you have learned from this chapter?

2. Where do you fall short according to this chapter?

3. What do you need to change according to this chapter?

_____

Questions regarding today's reading:

1. Who were the fisherman that began to follow Jesus?

2. Who was the tax-collector that began to follow Jesus?

3. Why were the Pharisees angry at Jesus regarding the Sabbath?

4. What habits do you need to develop according to this chapter?

4. Which unlikely people did Jesus tell us to love?

5. How can we know if a tree is good or bad?

Week 1; Day 4—Date _____
Luke 7-8
(In the space below, write any notes or thoughts you have regarding the text you are reading today.)

1. Write briefly what you have learned from this chapter?

2. Where do you fall short according to this chapter?

3. What do you need to change according to this chapter?

_____

Questions regarding today's reading:
1. What did Jesus find in the centurion that He had not even found in Israel?

2. Who did Jesus say is greater than John the Baptist?

3. Who loves more according to Jesus and the Pharisee?

4. What habits do you need to develop according to this chapter?

4. What does the seed produce when it is in good ground?

5. Name the ruler whose daughter Jesus raised?

Week 1; Day 5—Date _____
Luke 9-10
(In the space below, write any notes or thoughts you have regarding the text you are reading today.)

Thought Questions:

1. Write briefly what you have learned from this chapter?

2. Where do you fall short according to this chapter?

3. What do you need to change according to this chapter?

Questions regarding today's reading:

1. Who did the disciples believe Jesus was?

2. What must we do if we are to follow Christ?

3. For what should we pray since the harvest is plentiful?

4. What habits do you need to develop according to this chapter?

4. What two commandments must we follow to inherit eternal life?

5. Name the sisters who invited Jesus into their home.

Week 1—Group Discussion
Luke 1-10

1. What were the most important lessons you learned from this week's readings?

2. Which lessons from this week's readings had the most profound practical impact on your daily life?

3. What questions do you have about this week's readings?

4. What lessons from this week's readings do you need any help with?

5. What did Jesus do to combat each temptation in **Luke 4**? What does that say about how important it is for us to continue our habit of Bible study?

6. According to **Luke 6:20-26**, when are we blessed and when are we in trouble?

7. Jesus told Simon the Pharisee that the one who had been forgiven much would love much. How much have we been forgiven?

8. What does it mean for us to take up our crosses and follow Jesus?

Week 2; Day 1—Date _____
Luke 11-12

(In the space below, write any notes or thoughts you have regarding the text you are reading today.)

_____

Questions regarding today's reading:

1. About what did the disciples ask to be taught?

2. Upon what two groups did Jesus pronounce woes?

3. Why did Jesus say we ought to beware covetousness?

4. What should we seek instead of wealth?

5. What did Jesus say He was bringing instead of peace?

Thought Questions:

1. Write briefly what you have learned from this chapter?

2. Where do you fall short according to this chapter?

3. What do you need to change according to this chapter?

4. What habits do you need to develop according to this chapter?

Week 2; Day 2—Date _____
Luke 13-14

(In the space below, write any notes or thoughts you have regarding the text you are reading today.)

_____

Questions regarding today's reading:

1. What happens to those who do not repent?

2. To what two things did Jesus compare the kingdom?

3. What did Jerusalem do to the prophets sent to her?

4. Who cannot be Christ's disciples?

5. What is salt good for once it has lost its flavor?

Thought Questions:

1. Write briefly what you have learned from this chapter?

2. Where do you fall short according to this chapter?

3. What do you need to change according to this chapter?

4. What habits do you need to develop according to this chapter?

Week 2; Day 3—Date _____
Luke 15-16

(In the space below, write any notes or thoughts you have regarding the text you are reading today.)

Thought Questions:

1. Write briefly what you have learned from this chapter?

2. Where do you fall short according to this chapter?

3. What do you need to change according to this chapter?

Questions regarding today's reading:

1. What would a shepherd do if one of his sheep was lost?

2. How did the father treat the prodigal son when he returned?

3. If we are unfaithful in our use of money, will God entrust true riches to us?

4. What did Jesus call it if we divorce and marry someone else?

4. What habits do you need to develop according to this chapter?

5. What happened to Lazarus and the rich man when they died?

Week 2; Day 4—Date _____
Luke 17-18
(In the space below, write any notes or thoughts you have regarding the text you are reading today.)

_____

Questions regarding today's reading:
1. How often should we forgive those who sin against us?

2. How many of the healed lepers returned to thank Jesus?

3. Why was the tax collector justified?

4. What will we receive if we abandon all for the kingdom?

5. On what day would Jesus rise?

Week 2; Day 5—Date _____
Luke 19-20

(In the space below, write any notes or thoughts you have regarding the text you are reading today.)

_____

Questions regarding today's reading:

1. Who was the tax collector that repented at Jesus' teaching?

2. What would cry out if Jesus silenced the people as He entered Jerusalem?

3. In Jesus' parable, what did the vinedressers do to the owner's son?

4. What did Jesus say we should render to God when questioned about taxes?

5. Why were the disciples to beware of the scribes?

Thought Questions:

1. Write briefly what you have learned from this chapter?

2. Where do you fall short according to this chapter?

3. What do you need to change according to this chapter?

4. What habits do you need to develop according to this chapter?

Week 2—Group Discussion
Luke 11-20

1. What were the most important lessons you learned from this week's readings?

2. Which lessons from this week's readings had the most profound practical impact on your daily life?

3. What questions do you have about this week's readings?

4. What lessons from this week's readings do you need any help with?

5. Jesus taught the disciples to pray in **Luke 11**. Describe how we are to pray based on that teaching.

6. What do you think it means to seek God's kingdom?

7. How did the parable of the fig tree in **Luke 13** illustrate God's patience with us?

8. What comfort do the Parables of the Lost Sheep, Lost Coin and the Prodigal Son provide for us?

9. How did people know what to render to Caesar? Considering your answer to that question, how do we know what we are to render to God?

Week 3; Day 1—Date _____
Luke 21-22

(In the space below, write any notes or thoughts you have regarding the text you are reading today.)

Questions regarding today's reading:

1. According to Jesus, who pt the most into the temple treasury?

2. What was going to eventually happen to the temple?

3. Who sought to betray Jesus?

4. Who had asked to sift Simon Peter like wheat?

5. To whose house was Jesus taken after He was arrested?

Thought Questions:

1. Write briefly what you have learned from this chapter?

2. Where do you fall short according to this chapter?

3. What do you need to change according to this chapter?

4. What habits do you need to develop according to this chapter?

Week 3; Day 2—Date _____
Luke 23-24

(In the space below, write any notes or thoughts you have regarding the text you are reading today.)

_____

Questions regarding today's reading:

1. To whom did Pilate send Jesus?

2. Who helped bear Jesus' cross?

3. Into whose hand did Jesus commit His spirit?

4. Who ran to the tomb when the women reported Jesus' missing body?

5. What did Jesus do to demonstrate He was not just a spirit?

Thought Questions:

1. Write briefly what you have learned from this chapter?

2. Where do you fall short according to this chapter?

3. What do you need to change according to this chapter?

4. What habits do you need to develop according to this chapter?

Week 3; Day 3—Date _____
Acts 1-2

(In the space below, write any notes or thoughts you have regarding the text you are reading today.)

Thought Questions:

1. Write briefly what you have learned from this chapter?

2. Where do you fall short according to this chapter?

3. What do you need to change according to this chapter?

4. What habits do you need to develop according to this chapter?

Questions regarding today's reading:

1. How many disciples were gathering before Pentecost?

2. Who replaced Judas as an apostle?

3. According to **Acts 2:6-8**, what were the apostles doing when they were speaking "with other tongues?"

4. Where is David "to this day?"

5. How did those who believed Peter's preaching obey his teaching?

Week 3; Day 4—Date _____
Acts 3-4

(In the space below, write any notes or thoughts you have regarding the text you are reading today.)

_____

Questions regarding today's reading:

1. During what hour did Peter and John go to the temple to pray?

2. What will happen to those who refuse to hear the Prophet (Jesus)?

3. How many men were believers by **Acts 4:4**?

4. By whose name must we be saved?

5. What does Barnabas' name mean?

Thought Questions:

1. Write briefly what you have learned from this chapter?

2. Where do you fall short according to this chapter?

3. What do you need to change according to this chapter?

4. What habits do you need to develop according to this chapter?

Week 3; Day 5—Date _____
Acts 5-6

(In the space below, write any notes or thoughts you have regarding the text you are reading today.)

1. Write briefly what you have learned from this chapter?

2. Where do you fall short according to this chapter?

3. What do you need to change according to this chapter?

Questions regarding today's reading:

1. Why did fear come upon the church in **Acts 5:11**?

2. How did the apostles escape the common prison?

3. Why did Peter and the apostles preach the Gospel even though the Jews told them not to?

4. What habits do you need to develop according to this chapter?

4. Why were the Hellenistic widows complaining?

5. With whom did some from the Synagogue of the Freedmen dispute?

Week 3—Group Discussion
Luke 21-Acts 6

1. What were the most important lessons you learned from this week's readings?

2. Which lessons from this week's readings had the most profound practical impact on your daily life?

3. What questions do you have about this week's readings?

4. What lessons from this week's readings do you need any help with?

5. What do we learn about giving from the poor woman at the temple?

6. When Jesus prayed in the garden, what was His governing desire?

7. What do we learn about living with others from Jesus in **Luke 23:34**?

8. What governed the newly established church according to **Acts 2:42**? What does that say about the importance of continuing our habit of Bible study?

9. How could the apostles rejoice in suffering in **Acts 5:41**? How can we follow their example?

Week 4; Day 1—Date _____
Acts 7-8

(In the space below, write any notes or thoughts you have regarding the text you are reading today.)

Questions regarding today's reading:

1. What covenant did God give Abraham?

2. How did the Jews' fathers repeatedly respond to Moses and the prophets?

3. At whose feet did Stephen's stoners lay their clothes?

4. Who preached the gospel in Samaria, even converting a sorcerer?

5. What hindered the eunuch from being baptized?

Thought Questions:

1. Write briefly what you have learned from this chapter?

2. Where do you fall short according to this chapter?

3. What do you need to change according to this chapter?

4. What habits do you need to develop according to this chapter?

Week 4; Day 2—Date _____
Acts 9-10
(In the space below, write any notes or thoughts you have regarding the text you are reading today.)

Thought Questions:

1. Write briefly what you have learned from this chapter?

2. Where do you fall short according to this chapter?

3. What do you need to change according to this chapter?

4. What habits do you need to develop according to this chapter?

Questions regarding today's reading:

1. Why was Saul going to Damascus?

2. Whom did God send to teach Saul?

3. Who defended Saul to the apostles?

4. Name the Caesarean Centurion who became the first Gentile Christian?

5. How did Peter learn the Gentiles were also allowed salvation through water baptism?

Week 4; Day 3—Date _____
Acts 11-12

(In the space below, write any notes or thoughts you have regarding the text you are reading today.)

1. Write briefly what you have learned from this chapter?

2. Where do you fall short according to this chapter?

3. What do you need to change according to this chapter?

Questions regarding today's reading:

1. What had God also granted to the Gentiles?

2. According to **Acts 11:21**, why was the church in Antioch successful?

3. Who did the Jerusalem church send to strengthen the new Christians in Antioch?

4. What habits do you need to develop according to this chapter?

4. Who was the first martyred apostle?

5. At whose house were some disciples gathered to pray for Peter?

Week 4; Day 4—Date _____
Acts 13-14
(In the space below, write any notes or thoughts you have regarding the text you are reading today.)

Thought Questions:

1. Write briefly what you have learned from this chapter?

2. Where do you fall short according to this chapter?

3. What do you need to change according to this chapter?

4. What habits do you need to develop according to this chapter?

Questions regarding today's reading:

1. Whom did the Holy Spirit separate out among the teachers at Antioch?

2. Name the sorcerer who withstood Paul and Barnabas on Paphos.

3. Could the Law of Moses justify anyone?

4. Which pagan gods did the Lystrans believe Paul and Barnabas to be?

5. Through what must we enter the kingdom of God?

Week 4; Day 5—Date _____
Acts 15-16

(In the space below, write any notes or thoughts you have regarding the text you are reading today.)

Questions regarding today's reading:

1. What did the men from Judea claim the Gentiles had to do to be saved?

2. Whom did Jerusalem send with Paul and Barnabas to confirm the words of their letter?

3. Why did Paul and Barnabas separate ways?

4. Who was the first convert in Macedonia?

5. What did the jailer do immediately upon believing the gospel?

Thought Questions:

1. Write briefly what you have learned from this chapter?

2. Where do you fall short according to this chapter?

3. What do you need to change according to this chapter?

4. What habits do you need to develop according to this chapter?

Acts 7-16

1. What were the most important lessons you learned from this week's readings?

2. Which lessons from this week's readings had the most profound practical impact on your daily life?

3. What questions do you have about this week's readings?

4. What lessons from this week's readings do you need any help with?

5. What did the brethren who were scattered from Jerusalem do? How can we follow their example?

6. Why is Saul's conversion such an amazing testimony to the Gospel's truth?

7. What example did Mary, the mother of John Mark, set for us in **Acts 12:12**?

8. In **Acts 15**, what three arguments convinced the brethren that Gentiles did not have to be circumcised to become Christians?

9. What do we learn about personal evangelism from Paul in **Acts 16**?

Week 5; Day 1—Date _____
Acts 17-18

(In the space below, write any notes or thoughts you have regarding the text you are reading today.)

2. Where do you fall short according to this chapter?

3. What do you need to change according to this chapter?

Questions regarding today's reading:

1. In Thessalonica, whom did the Jews drag to the rulers of the city?

2. Why was Luke impressed with the Bereans above the Thessalonians?

3. Which religious inscription did Paul bring to the Athenians attention?

4. What habits do you need to develop according to this chapter?

4. Who were the two tentmakers that Paul met in Corinth?

5. What did Aquila and Priscilla have to correct with Apollos?

Week 5; Day 2—Date _____
Acts 19-20

(In the space below, write any notes or thoughts you have regarding the text you are reading today.)

1. Write briefly what you have learned from this chapter?

2. Where do you fall short according to this chapter?

3. What do you need to change according to this chapter?

_____

Questions regarding today's reading:

1. Why did Paul have to baptize the 12 Ephesians again?

2. Name the silversmith who caused a riot in Ephesus?

3. When did the disciples gather to "break bread?"

4. What habits do you need to develop according to this chapter?

4. What was awaiting Paul in Jerusalem?

5. To what did Paul commend the Ephesian elders?

Week 5; Day 3—Date _____
Acts 21-22

(In the space below, write any notes or thoughts you have regarding the text you are reading today.)

1. Write briefly what you have learned from this chapter?

2. Where do you fall short according to this chapter?

3. What do you need to change according to this chapter?

Questions regarding today's reading:

1. What did Agabus prophesy about Paul?

2. Who did the Roman commander initially believe Paul to be?

3. Who had been Paul's teacher when he was younger?

4. When were Paul's sins washed away?

5. How had Paul become a Roman citizen?

4. What habits do you need to develop according to this chapter?

Week 5; Day 4—Date _____
Acts 23-24
(In the space below, write any notes or thoughts you have regarding the text you are reading today.)

Thought Questions:
1. Write briefly what you have learned from this chapter?

2. Where do you fall short according to this chapter?

3. What do you need to change according to this chapter?

4. What habits do you need to develop according to this chapter?

Questions regarding today's reading:
1. How did Paul cause an argument among the Jewish council?

2. Who overheard and informed Paul of the plot on his life?

3. To what governor was Paul sent?

4. Why did Felix often speak with Paul?

5. Why did Felix leave Paul imprisoned when Festus succeeded him?

Week 5; Day 5—Date _____
Acts 25-26

(In the space below, write any notes or thoughts you have regarding the text you are reading today.)

Thought Questions:
1. Write briefly what you have learned from this chapter?

2. Where do you fall short according to this chapter?

3. What do you need to change according to this chapter?

4. What habits do you need to develop according to this chapter?

Questions regarding today's reading:

1. Who replaced Felix as governor?

2. To whom did Paul appeal for judgment?

3. What king visited Festus and wanted to hear Paul?

4. When Jesus had appeared to Paul, whom did He claim Paul was actually persecuting?

5. What was Agrippa's response to Paul's teaching?

Week 5—Group Discussion
Acts 17-26

1. What were the most important lessons you learned from this week's readings?

2. Which lessons from this week's readings had the most profound practical impact on your daily life?

3. What questions do you have about this week's readings?

4. What lessons from this week's readings do you need any help with?

5. If we want to be fair-minded (noble-minded) like the Bereans, what must we do?

6. What do we learn about God from Paul's sermon in **Acts 17:22-31**?

7. Based on **Acts 22:12-16**, at what point did Paul receive forgiveness?

8. According to **Acts 24:14**, why did Paul follow the Way?

9. Is being almost persuaded to become a Christian enough to be forgiven? Explain your answer.

Week 6; Day 1—Date _____
Acts 27-28

(In the space below, write any notes or thoughts you have regarding the text you are reading today.)

Questions regarding today's reading:

1. Name the centurion to whom Paul was entrusted to get to Rome.

2. How many died in the shipwreck on Malta?

3. Name the leading citizen of Malta?

4. Why did the Roman Jews want to hear from Paul?

5. Though Paul was under house arrest, what was he freely doing?

Thought Questions:

1. Write briefly what you have learned from this chapter?

2. Where do you fall short according to this chapter?

3. What do you need to change according to this chapter?

4. What habits do you need to develop according to this chapter?

Week 6; Day 2—Date _____
Romans 1-2

(In the space below, write any notes or thoughts you have regarding the text you are reading today.)

_____

Questions regarding today's reading:

1. Who wrote the letter to the Romans?

2. Of what was Paul unashamed?

3. To what does the kindness of God lead?

4. To whom is God partial?

5. From whom should our praise come?

Thought Questions:

1. Write briefly what you have learned from this chapter?

2. Where do you fall short according to this chapter?

3. What do you need to change according to this chapter?

4. What habits do you need to develop according to this chapter?

Week 6; Day 3—Date _____
Romans 3-4

(In the space below, write any notes or thoughts you have regarding the text you are reading today.)

Questions regarding today's reading:

1. Who has been charged with being under sin?

2. How many people will be justified by the works of the law?

3. When was Abraham's faith credited to him as righteousness?

4. Of whom is Abraham the father?

5. Of what was Abraham assured regarding God's promises?

Thought Questions:

1. Write briefly what you have learned from this chapter?

2. Where do you fall short according to this chapter?

3. What do you need to change according to this chapter?

4. What habits do you need to develop according to this chapter?

Week 6; Day 4—Date _____
Romans 5-6
(In the space below, write any notes or thoughts you have regarding the text you are reading today.)

Thought Questions:

1. Write briefly what you have learned from this chapter?

2. Where do you fall short according to this chapter?

3. What do you need to change according to this chapter?

4. What habits do you need to develop according to this chapter?

Questions regarding today's reading:

1. What does tribulation ultimately produce?

2. When did Christ die for the ungodly?

3. What happened when sin increased?

4. Should we sin so that grace may abound?

5. What are the wages of sin and the gift of God?

Week 6; Day 5—Date _____
Romans 7-8

(In the space below, write any notes or thoughts you have regarding the text you are reading today.)

Questions regarding today's reading:

1. How long does the law have jurisdiction over a person?

2. What became a cause of death for Paul?

3. Where is there no condemnation?

4. Who are the sons of God?

5. What can separate us from the love of God in Christ Jesus?

Thought Questions:

1. Write briefly what you have learned from this chapter?

2. Where do you fall short according to this chapter?

3. What do you need to change according to this chapter?

4. What habits do you need to develop according to this chapter?

Week 6—Group Discussion
Acts 27-Romans 8

1. What were the most important lessons you learned from this week's readings?

2. Which lessons from this week's readings had the most profound practical impact on your daily life?

3. What questions do you have about this week's readings?

4. What lessons from this week's readings do you need any help with?

5. According to **Acts 28:22**, what can we expect people in the world and even in other religions to say about us?

6. Why was Paul unashamed of the Gospel of Jesus Christ?

7. According to **Romans 3:23**, what is the standard regarding sin and righteousness?

8. In **Romans 5:3-5**, Paul said tribulation produces hope. How does that happen?

9. Reading through **Romans 6**, how should the Christian relate to sin?

Week 7; Day 1—Date _____
Romans 9-10

(In the space below, write any notes or thoughts you have regarding the text you are reading today.)

Thought Questions:

1. Write briefly what you have learned from this chapter?

2. Where do you fall short according to this chapter?

3. What do you need to change according to this chapter?

4. What habits do you need to develop according to this chapter?

Questions regarding today's reading:

1. Who are regarded as the children of God?

2. Upon whom will God have mercy?

3. What was Paul's desire and prayer for the Jews?

4. What distinction is there between the Jew and the Greek?

5. From where does faith come?

Week 7; Day 2—Date _____
Romans 11-12

(In the space below, write any notes or thoughts you have regarding the text you are reading today.)

Thought Questions:

1. Write briefly what you have learned from this chapter?

2. Where do you fall short according to this chapter?

3. What do you need to change according to this chapter?

Questions regarding today's reading:

1. How many had God kept for Himself who had not bowed their knee to Baal?

2. Why has God shut up all under disobedience?

3. In what way are we to present our bodies to God?

4. Who are we to bless?

5. When are we allowed to take our own revenge?

4. What habits do you need to develop according to this chapter?

Week 7; Day 3—Date _____
Romans 13-14

(In the space below, write any notes or thoughts you have regarding the text you are reading today.)

Thought Questions:

1. Write briefly what you have learned from this chapter?

2. Where do you fall short according to this chapter?

3. What do you need to change according to this chapter?

4. What habits do you need to develop according to this chapter?

Questions regarding today's reading:

1. From where do the governing authorities come?

2. What is the fulfillment of the law?

3. How many provisions are we allowed to make for the lusts of the flesh?

4. For whom are we to live or die?

5. If we doubt or act without faith, what have we done?

Week 7; Day 4—Date _____
Romans 15-16
(In the space below, write any notes or thoughts you have regarding the text you are reading today.)

Thought Questions:
1. Write briefly what you have learned from this chapter?

2. Where do you fall short according to this chapter?

3. What do you need to change according to this chapter?

4. What habits do you need to develop according to this chapter?

Questions regarding today's reading:
1. Why were the things written in earlier times written?

2. Where did Paul want the Romans to help him travel?

3. Who was the first Asian convert?

4. Who are we to mark or keep an eye on?

5. According to what will God establish us?

Week 7; Day 5—Date _____
Galatians 1-2
(In the space below, write any notes or thoughts you have regarding the text you are reading today.)

Questions regarding today's reading:

1. From whom was Paul sent as an apostle?

2. How did Paul receive the gospel he preached?

3. How long did Paul yield in subjection to the false brethren?

4. Who did Paul oppose or withstand when he came to Antioch?

5. With whom are we to be crucified?

Thought Questions:

1. Write briefly what you have learned from this chapter?

2. Where do you fall short according to this chapter?

3. What do you need to change according to this chapter?

4. What habits do you need to develop according to this chapter?

Week 7—Group Discussion
Romans 9-Galatians 2

1. What were the most important lessons you learned from this week's readings?

2. Which lessons from this week's readings had the most profound practical impact on your daily life?

3. What questions do you have about this week's readings?

4. What lessons from this week's readings do you need any help with?

5. According to **Romans 10:13-15**, what must we do if people are going to be saved?

6. What are the two aspects of God that we must always balance out as we determine how we are going to live?

7. Describe the Christians life according to **Romans 12**?

8. What are the strong supposed to do for the weak according to the beginning of **Romans 15**?

9. What does it mean to be crucified with Christ?

Week 8; Day 1—Date _____
Galatians 3-4
(In the space below, write any notes or thoughts you have regarding the text you are reading today.)

1. Write briefly what you have learned from this chapter?

2. Where do you fall short according to this chapter?

3. What do you need to change according to this chapter?

Questions regarding today's reading:

1. Who are the sons of Abraham?

2. How are we clothed in Christ?

3. Why had Paul preached to the Galatians the first time?

4. What habits do you need to develop according to this chapter?

4. What had the Galatians been willing to pluck out and give to Paul?

5. What do those born of the flesh do to those born according to the Spirit?

Week 8; Day 2—Date _____
Galatians 5-6
(In the space below, write any notes or thoughts you have regarding the text you are reading today.)

Thought Questions:

1. Write briefly what you have learned from this chapter?

2. Where do you fall short according to this chapter?

3. What do you need to change according to this chapter?

4. What habits do you need to develop according to this chapter?

_____

Questions regarding today's reading:

1. Who has been severed from Christ and fallen from grace?

2. In what statement is the whole law fulfilled?

3. What are the fruit of the Spirit?

4. With what kind of spirit are we to restore someone?

5. In what alone would Paul boast?

Week 8; Day 3—Date _____
Ephesians 1-2

(In the space below, write any notes or thoughts you have regarding the text you are reading today.)

Thought Questions:

1. Write briefly what you have learned from this chapter?

2. Where do you fall short according to this chapter?

3. What do you need to change according to this chapter?

Questions regarding today's reading:

1. Who wrote the letter to the Ephesians?

2. What is Jesus head over?

3. According to what course did we all formerly walk?

4. By what have we been saved?

5. Who is the chief corner stone of God's household?

4. What habits do you need to develop according to this chapter?

Week 8; Day 4—Date _____

Ephesians 3-4

(In the space below, write any notes or thoughts you have regarding the text you are reading today.)

_____

Questions regarding today's reading:

1. Through what is the wisdom of God being made known to rulers and authorities in heavenly places?

2. What is God able to do according to the power that works in us?

3. How does Paul describe the unity we must pursue?

4. What is the whole body held together by?

5. What must we put off and what must we put on?

Thought Questions:

1. Write briefly what you have learned from this chapter?

2. Where do you fall short according to this chapter?

3. What do you need to change according to this chapter?

4. What habits do you need to develop according to this chapter?

56

Week 8; Day 5—Date _____
Ephesians 5-6

(In the space below, write any notes or thoughts you have regarding the text you are reading today.)

Thought Questions:

1. Write briefly what you have learned from this chapter?

2. Where do you fall short according to this chapter?

3. What do you need to change according to this chapter?

4. What habits do you need to develop according to this chapter?

Questions regarding today's reading:

1. Who must we imitate?

2. What does Paul call the covetous man?

3. How are husbands to love their wives?

4. What is the sword of the Spirit?

5. Whom did Paul send to let the Ephesians know of his circumstances?

Week 8—Group Discussion
Galatians 3-Ephesian 6

1. What were the most important lessons you learned from this week's readings?

2. Which lessons from this week's readings had the most profound practical impact on your daily life?

3. What questions do you have about this week's readings?

4. What lessons from this week's readings do you need any help with?

5. Compare the works of the flesh to the fruit of the Spirit.

6. According to **Ephesians 1**, what blessings do we have in Christ Jesus?

7. What are the standards of unity?

8. Describe the new person that Christians are to become based on **Ephesians 4-5**.

9. Describe the armor of God.

Week 9; Day 1—Date _____
Philippians 1-2

(In the space below, write any notes or thoughts you have regarding the text you are reading today.)

Questions regarding today's reading:

1. To whom did Paul and Timothy write this letter?

2. What had been granted to the Philippians for Christ's sake?

3. How were the Philippians to regard one another?

4. Who did Paul hope to send to the Philippians shortly?

5. Who had Paul already sent to the Philippians?

Thought Questions:

1. Write briefly what you have learned from this chapter?

2. Where do you fall short according to this chapter?

3. What do you need to change according to this chapter?

4. What habits do you need to develop according to this chapter?

Week 9; Day 2—Date _____
Philippians 3-4
(In the space below, write any notes or thoughts you have regarding the text you are reading today.)

_____

Questions regarding today's reading:

1. Of whom were the Philippians to beware?

2. To what did Paul press on?

3. Where is the Christian's citizenship?

4. What things did Paul tell the Philippians to practice?

5. In whose household does Paul say there are saints?

Thought Questions:

1. Write briefly what you have learned from this chapter?

2. Where do you fall short according to this chapter?

3. What do you need to change according to this chapter?

4. What habits do you need to develop according to this chapter?

Week 9; Day 3—Date _____
Colossians 1-2

(In the space below, write any notes or thoughts you have regarding the text you are reading today.)

1. Write briefly what you have learned from this chapter?

2. Where do you fall short according to this chapter?

3. What do you need to change according to this chapter?

Questions regarding today's reading:

1. Who wrote this letter?

2. Into what has the Father transferred us?

3. What dwells in Christ in bodily form?

4. When were we buried with Christ?

4. What habits do you need to develop according to this chapter?

5. Regarding what must we not let others act as our judge?

Week 9; Day 4—Date _____

Colossians 3-4

(In the space below, write any notes or thoughts you have regarding the text you are reading today.)

Thought Questions:

1. Write briefly what you have learned from this chapter?

2. Where do you fall short according to this chapter?

3. What do you need to change according to this chapter?

4. What habits do you need to develop according to this chapter?

Questions regarding today's reading:

1. Where must we set our minds?

2. What is the perfect bond of unity?

3. What is the children's responsibility in the home?

4. Who would inform the Colossians of Paul's affairs?

5. In what other church was this letter to be read?

Week 9; Day 5—Date _____
Mark 1-2
(In the space below, write any notes or thoughts you have regarding the text you are reading today.)

Questions regarding today's reading:
1. What did John the Baptist preach?

2. What did Jesus promise to make Simon and Andrew?

3. Why did Jesus go to a secluded place in the early morning?

4. What did Jesus tell Levi, the son of Alphaeus to do?

5. Who is Lord of the Sabbath?

Thought Questions:
1. Write briefly what you have learned from this chapter?

2. Where do you fall short according to this chapter?

3. What do you need to change according to this chapter?

4. What habits do you need to develop according to this chapter?

Week 9—Group Discussion
Philippians 1-Mark 2

1. What were the most important lessons you learned from this week's readings?

2. Which lessons from this week's readings had the most profound practical impact on your daily life?

3. What questions do you have about this week's readings?

4. What lessons from this week's readings do you need any help with?

5. What did you learn from the book of **Philippians** about how to live with joy, even in the face of hardship?

6. How did Paul encourage us to overcome anxiety in the book of **Philippians**?

7. **Colossians 1:6** spoke of the word bearing fruit throughout the world. What does that mean?

8. How is love the perfect bond of unity? How can we improve love in our own lives?

9. What hinders most Christians from being fishers of men? How can we improve our own fishing skills?

Week 10; Day 1—Date _____
Mark 3-4

(In the space below, write any notes or thoughts you have regarding the text you are reading today.)

Thought Questions:
1. Write briefly what you have learned from this chapter?

2. Where do you fall short according to this chapter?

3. What do you need to change according to this chapter?

Questions regarding today's reading:

1. What would the unclean spirits say when they saw Jesus?

2. Who did Jesus claim were His mother and His brothers?

3. What must those who have ears to hear do?

4. To whom did Jesus explain His parables?

5. Where was Jesus when the storm rocked the boat?

4. What habits do you need to develop according to this chapter?

Week 10; Day 2—Date _____
Mark 5-6

(In the space below, write any notes or thoughts you have regarding the text you are reading today.)

Thought Questions:

1. Write briefly what you have learned from this chapter?

2. Where do you fall short according to this chapter?

3. What do you need to change according to this chapter?

4. What habits do you need to develop according to this chapter?

_____

Questions regarding today's reading:

1. What was the name of the unclean spirit?

2. What did Jesus want the previously demon-possessed man to do?

3. Who did Jesus allow to accompany him to the house of the synagogue official?

4. Who were Jesus' physical brothers?

5. How many baskets of scraps did the apostles pick up after Jesus fed the crowd?

Week 10; Day 3—Date _____
Mark 7-8

(In the space below, write any notes or thoughts you have regarding the text you are reading today.)

Questions regarding today's reading:

1. Who prophesied of people who honor God with their lips?

2. What did the Syrophoenician woman want Jesus to do?

3. With how many loaves did Jesus feed the four thousand?

4. Of what did Jesus tell His disciples to beware?

5. Who did Peter say Jesus was?

Thought Questions:

1. Write briefly what you have learned from this chapter?

2. Where do you fall short according to this chapter?

3. What do you need to change according to this chapter?

4. What habits do you need to develop according to this chapter?

Week 10; Day 4—Date _____
Mark 9-10

(In the space below, write any notes or thoughts you have regarding the text you are reading today.)

Thought Questions:

1. Write briefly what you have learned from this chapter?

2. Where do you fall short according to this chapter?

3. What do you need to change according to this chapter?

4. What habits do you need to develop according to this chapter?

Questions regarding today's reading:

1. Which disciples witnessed Jesus' transfiguration?

2. What must we do to be first according to Jesus?

3. To whom does the kingdom of God belong?

4. What did James and John want Jesus to grant them?

5. What did Bartimaeus cry out when Jesus passed by?

Week 10; Day 5—Date _____
Mark 11-12

(In the space below, write any notes or thoughts you have regarding the text you are reading today.)

Questions regarding today's reading:

1. What did those who surrounded Jesus as He entered Jerusalem shout?

2. What must we do for others if we wish God to forgive us?

3. What were they to render to Caesar? ... to God?

4. For what reason did Jesus say the Sadducees were mistaken?

5. Who did Jesus say had put the most in the temple treasury?

Thought Questions:

1. Write briefly what you have learned from this chapter?

2. Where do you fall short according to this chapter?

3. What do you need to change according to this chapter?

4. What habits do you need to develop according to this chapter?

69

Week 10—Group Discussion
Mark 3-12

1. What were the most important lessons you learned from this week's readings?

2. Which lessons from this week's readings had the most profound practical impact on your daily life?

3. What questions do you have about this week's readings?

4. What lessons from this week's readings do you need any help with?

5. What did you learn from the parable of the sower?

6. Explain how we will follow the teaching of **Mark 9:42-50** on a practical level?

7. How long did Jesus expect people to remain married? How can we ensure we obey this teaching?

8. In **Mark 9** and **10**, Jesus says a lot about serving. How can we be the kind of servant Jesus teaches about?

9. How important to our salvation is that we forgive others? How can we accomplish this?

Week 11; Day 1—Date _____
Mark 13-14

(In the space below, write any notes or thoughts you have regarding the text you are reading today.)

Thought Questions:

1. Write briefly what you have learned from this chapter?

2. Where do you fall short according to this chapter?

3. What do you need to change according to this chapter?

4. What habits do you need to develop according to this chapter?

Questions regarding today's reading:

1. What was going to happen to the buildings of Jerusalem?

2. What were the chief priests and scribes seeking to do with Jesus?

3. Who went out to the chief priests in order to betray Jesus?

4. When would Jesus drink the fruit of the vine again?

5. What did Peter do when he remembered Jesus' words about his denials?

Week 11; Day 2—Date _____
Mark 15-16

(In the space below, write any notes or thoughts you have regarding the text you are reading today.)

Thought Questions:

1. Write briefly what you have learned from this chapter?

2. Where do you fall short according to this chapter?

3. What do you need to change according to this chapter?

4. What habits do you need to develop according to this chapter?

Questions regarding today's reading:

1. To whom did the priests, elders and scribes deliver Jesus?

2. Who bore the cross of Jesus?

3. Who asked Pilate for the body of Jesus?

4. What were the women to tell Peter and the disciples?

5. Why did Jesus reproach and rebuke the disciples when He appeared to them?

Week 11; Day 3—Date _____
I Peter 1-2

(In the space below, write any notes or thoughts you have regarding the text you are reading today.)

Questions regarding today's reading:

1. How has God caused us to be born again to a living hope?

2. Why are we to be holy?

3. What must we long for like newborn babes?

4. To whom are we to submit ourselves for the Lord's sake?

5. How were we healed?

Thought Questions:

1. Write briefly what you have learned from this chapter?

2. Where do you fall short according to this chapter?

3. What do you need to change according to this chapter?

4. What habits do you need to develop according to this chapter?

Week 11; Day 4—Date _____
I Peter 3-4

(In the space below, write any notes or thoughts you have regarding the text you are reading today.)

Thought Questions:

1. Write briefly what you have learned from this chapter?

2. Where do you fall short according to this chapter?

3. What do you need to change according to this chapter?

Questions regarding today's reading:

1. How may disobedient husbands be won by their wives?

2. How many times did Christ die for sins?

3. Why are the Gentiles surprised with us?

4. What habits do you need to develop according to this chapter?

4. What does love cover?

5. What should those do who suffer as a Christian?

Week 11; Day 5—Date _____
I Peter 5-II Peter 1

(In the space below, write any notes or thoughts you have regarding the text you are reading today.)

Thought Questions:
1. Write briefly what you have learned from this chapter?

2. Where do you fall short according to this chapter?

3. What do you need to change according to this chapter?

4. What habits do you need to develop according to this chapter?

Questions regarding today's reading:
1. Who were the elders to shepherd?

2. What will God do for us after we have suffered for Him for a little while?

3. In what will grace and peace be multiplied to us?

4. Of what must we be diligent to make sure?

5. How should we pay attention to the prophetic word?

Week 11—Group Discussion
Mark 13-II Peter 1

1. What were the most important lessons you learned from this week's readings?

2. Which lessons from this week's readings had the most profound practical impact on your daily life?

3. What questions do you have about this week's readings?

4. What lessons from this week's readings do you need any help with?

5. What does the crucifixion mean to you?

6. How is Jesus both a cornerstone and a stumbling stone? How can we make sure He is our cornerstone and not our stumbling stone?

7. **I Peter** says a great deal about suffering. What did you learn about Christian's suffering from that letter?

8. Describe how Christians should relate to one another and to folks in the world according to **I Peter**?

9. What did you learn about growing in Christ from **II Peter 1:5-11**?

Week 12; Day 1—Date _____
II Peter 2-3

(In the space below, write any notes or thoughts you have regarding the text you are reading today.)

1. Write briefly what you have learned from this chapter?

2. Where do you fall short according to this chapter?

3. What do you need to change according to this chapter?

Questions regarding today's reading:

1. Who did God preserve when He destroyed the ancient world by flood?

2. What did Balaam love?

3. Whose words does Peter want us to remember?

4. Why is the Lord patient with us?

5. What do the untaught and the unstable do with the writings of Paul and the rest of the scripture?

4. What habits do you need to develop according to this chapter?

Week 12; Day 2—Date _____
Jude-I Corinthians 1

(In the space below, write any notes or thoughts you have regarding the text you are reading today.)

Questions regarding today's reading:

1. What was Jude making every effort to write about?

2. What did Enoch prophecy in the seventh generation from Adam?

3. Who is able to keep us from stumbling?

4. Who wrote the letter to the Corinthians?

5. What does Paul say he preaches which is foolishness to Gentiles and stumbling block to Jews?

Thought Questions:

1. Write briefly what you have learned from this chapter?

2. Where do you fall short according to this chapter?

3. What do you need to change according to this chapter?

4. What habits do you need to develop according to this chapter?

Week 12; Day 3—Date _____
I Corinthians 2-3

(In the space below, write any notes or thoughts you have regarding the text you are reading today.)

Questions regarding today's reading:

1. Upon what did Paul want the faith of the Corinthians to rest?

2. What spirit did Paul claim to have received?

3. What did Paul say he and Apollos were?

4. Who causes the growth?

5. Who should boast in men?

Thought Questions:

1. Write briefly what you have learned from this chapter?

2. Where do you fall short according to this chapter?

3. What do you need to change according to this chapter?

4. What habits do you need to develop according to this chapter?

Week 12; Day 4—Date _____
I Corinthians 4-5
(In the space below, write any notes or thoughts you have regarding the text you are reading today.)

_____

Questions regarding today's reading:

1. What is required of stewards?

2. Who had Paul sent to the Corinthians?

3. What had been reported to Paul about the Corinthians?

4. To whom were the Corinthians to deliver the immoral brother?

5. With what are we to celebrate our "Passover Feast"?

Thought Questions:

1. Write briefly what you have learned from this chapter?

2. Where do you fall short according to this chapter?

3. What do you need to change according to this chapter?

4. What habits do you need to develop according to this chapter?

Week 12; Day 5—Date _____
I Corinthians 6-7

(In the space below, write any notes or thoughts you have regarding the text you are reading today.)

Thought Questions:

1. Write briefly what you have learned from this chapter?

2. Where do you fall short according to this chapter?

3. What do you need to change according to this chapter?

4. What habits do you need to develop according to this chapter?

Questions regarding today's reading:

1. According to Paul, who will judge the world and angels?

2. Who will not inherit the kingdom of God?

3. What must we do with our bodies since we have been bought with a price?

4. What is the one who is unmarried concerned about?

5. What is the one who is married concerned about?

Week 12—Group Discussion
II Peter 2-I Corinthians 7

1. What were the most important lessons you learned from this week's readings?

2. Which lessons from this week's readings had the most profound practical impact on your daily life?

3. What questions do you have about this week's readings?

4. What lessons from this week's readings do you need any help with?

5. How do the false teachers entice us to enter sin again?

6. What will our lives look like if we are preparing each day for Christ's return and judgment?

7. What did you learn about wisdom and foolishness from Paul in **I Corinthians**?

8. If men are doing to the teaching, how does God cause the growth?

9. What does Paul teach about marriage in **I Corinthians 7**?

Week 13; Day 1—Date _____
I Corinthians 8-9

(In the space below, write any notes or thoughts you have regarding the text you are reading today.)

Questions regarding today's reading:

1. What does knowledge do? What does love do?

2. What did the Law say about muzzling the ox?

3. Why did Paul not use his rights but endure all things?

4. Why did Paul make himself a slave to all men?

5. Why did Paul discipline his body?

Thought Questions:

1. Write briefly what you have learned from this chapter?

2. Where do you fall short according to this chapter?

3. What do you need to change according to this chapter?

4. What habits do you need to develop according to this chapter?

Week 13; Day 2—Date _____
I Corinthians 10-11

(In the space below, write any notes or thoughts you have regarding the text you are reading today.)

_____

Questions regarding today's reading:

1. From what rock did Paul claim the Israelites were drinking?

2. Whose good are we to seek?

3. Why did Paul praise the Corinthians?

4. What problem existed among the Corinthian church?

5. If anyone is hungry, where should they eat?

Thought Questions:

1. Write briefly what you have learned from this chapter?

2. Where do you fall short according to this chapter?

3. What do you need to change according to this chapter?

4. What habits do you need to develop according to this chapter?

Week 13; Day 3—Date _____
I Corinthians 12-13

(In the space below, write any notes or thoughts you have regarding the text you are reading today.)

Thought Questions:

1. Write briefly what you have learned from this chapter?

2. Where do you fall short according to this chapter?

3. What do you need to change according to this chapter?

4. What habits do you need to develop according to this chapter?

Questions regarding today's reading:

1. For what purpose was each person given a manifestation of the Spirit?

2. Where has God placed each member of the body?

3. What happens when one member of the body suffers or is honored?

4. What is love?

5. What is the greatest—faith, hope or love?

Week 13; Day 4—Date _____
I Corinthians 14-15

(In the space below, write any notes or thoughts you have regarding the text you are reading today.)

_____

Questions regarding today's reading:

1. For what purpose does one who prophesies speak to men?

2. In what must we be infants? In what must we be mature?

3. How must all things be done in the congregational worship?

4. Who is the first fruits of the dead or of those who are asleep?

5. Through whom does God give us the victory?

Thought Questions:

1. Write briefly what you have learned from this chapter?

2. Where do you fall short according to this chapter?

3. What do you need to change according to this chapter?

4. What habits do you need to develop according to this chapter?

Week 13; Day 5—Date _____
I Corinthians 16-II Corinthians 1
(In the space below, write any notes or thoughts you have regarding the text you are reading today.)

Thought Questions:

1. Write briefly what you have learned from this chapter?

2. Where do you fall short according to this chapter?

3. What do you need to change according to this chapter?

_____

Questions regarding today's reading:

1. Where would Paul travel before coming to the Corinthians?

2. Whose household were the first fruits of Achaia?

3. Why does God comfort us in our afflictions?

4. What habits do you need to develop according to this chapter?

4. How had Paul, Silvanus and Timothy conducted themselves in the world?

5. In whom does God establish us?

Week 13—Group Discussion
I Corinthians 8-II Corinthians 1

1. What were the most important lessons you learned from this week's readings?

2. Which lessons from this week's readings had the most profound practical impact on your daily life?

3. What questions do you have about this week's readings?

4. What lessons from this week's readings do you need any help with?

5. In **I Corinthians 9:24-27**, Paul related being a Christian to running a race. What similarities do you see between running a race and being a Christian? Considering that comparison what do we need to do to be able to run the Christian race better?

6. In **I Corinthians 10**, Paul said the Old Testament characters and narratives were given to us as examples. What are your favorite Old Testament characters or narratives and what examples do you learn from them?

7. What practical lessons about relationships in the congregation did you learn from **I Corinthians 12**?

8. Why is the resurrection so important for modern Christians? Why is it important to you personally?

9. In **II Corinthians 1:20**, Paul talked about the firm promises of God. How do God's promises provide you with comfort?

Week 14; Day 1—Date _____
II Corinthians 2-3

(In the space below, write any notes or thoughts you have regarding the text you are reading today.)

Thought Questions:

1. Write briefly what you have learned from this chapter?

2. Where do you fall short according to this chapter?

3. What do you need to change according to this chapter?

4. What habits do you need to develop according to this chapter?

Questions regarding today's reading:

1. Why had Paul written to the Corinthians earlier with many tears?

2. Where was a door opened for Paul in the Lord?

3. Who did Paul claim was his letter of commendation?

4. Who used to put a veil over his face?

5. When is the veil taken away from our hearts?

Week 14; Day 2—Date _____
II Corinthians 4-5
(In the space below, write any notes or thoughts you have regarding the text you are reading today.)

1. Write briefly what you have learned from this chapter?

2. Where do you fall short according to this chapter?

3. What do you need to change according to this chapter?

Questions regarding today's reading:

1. Who did Paul say had shone in his heart to give the Light of knowledge?

2. For what reason did Paul speak?

3. How should we walk?

4. What reason did Paul persuade men?

5. What did God make Him who knew no sin?

4. What habits do you need to develop according to this chapter?

Week 14; Day 3—Date _____
II Corinthians 6-7

(In the space below, write any notes or thoughts you have regarding the text you are reading today.)

Questions regarding today's reading:

1. When is the acceptable time and the day of salvation?

2. Whose temple are we Christians?

3. With whose coming did God comfort Paul?

4. What produces a repentance without regret?

5. How did the Corinthians receive Titus?

Thought Questions:

1. Write briefly what you have learned from this chapter?

2. Where do you fall short according to this chapter?

3. What do you need to change according to this chapter?

4. What habits do you need to develop according to this chapter?

Week 14; Day 4—Date _____
II Corinthians 8-9

(In the space below, write any notes or thoughts you have regarding the text you are reading today.)

Thought Questions:

1. Write briefly what you have learned from this chapter?

2. Where do you fall short according to this chapter?

3. What do you need to change according to this chapter?

4. What habits do you need to develop according to this chapter?

Questions regarding today's reading:

1. To whom did the churches of Macedonia first give themselves?

2. In whose sight did Paul have regard for what was honorable?

3. Who will reap sparingly? …bountifully?

4. How must each person give?

5. Why would God make all grace abound to the Corinthian brethren?

Week 14; Day 5—Date _____
II Corinthians 10-11

(In the space below, write any notes or thoughts you have regarding the text you are reading today.)

Thought Questions:
1. Write briefly what you have learned from this chapter?

2. Where do you fall short according to this chapter?

3. What do you need to change according to this chapter?

4. What habits do you need to develop according to this chapter?

Questions regarding today's reading:
1. What are the weapons of Paul's warfare?

2. In whom should we boast?

3. Who did Paul rob to serve the Corinthians?

4. How does Satan disguise himself?

5. How did Paul escape from Damascus?

Week 14—Group Discussion
II Corinthians 2-11

1. What were the most important lessons you learned from this week's readings?

2. Which lessons from this week's readings had the most profound practical impact on your daily life?

3. What questions do you have about this week's readings?

4. What lessons from this week's readings do you need any help with?

5. In **II Corinthians 5:7**, Paul spoke of walking by faith and not by sight. What does that mean and how do we know when we are doing it?

6. What is real repentance according to **II Corinthians 7** and how should we treat those who have repented? Why is that hard sometimes? What advice would you give to help us treat our penitent brethren properly?

7. Paul said the Macedonians did so much to help their brethren in need because they had given themselves to God first (**II Corinthians 8:5**). How do we give ourselves to God? Why does that improve all our relationships?

8. How can we be cheerful givers? (not only to the Lord but also to other people)

Week 15; Day 1—Date _____
II Corinthians 12-13

(In the space below, write any notes or thoughts you have regarding the text you are reading today.)

Questions regarding today's reading:

1. Why did God give Paul a thorn in the flesh?

2. When did Paul say he was strong?

3. Over what was Paul afraid he would mourn when he came to Corinth?

4. How many witnesses confirmed every fact?

5. For what purpose did God give Paul authority?

Thought Questions:

1. Write briefly what you have learned from this chapter?

2. Where do you fall short according to this chapter?

3. What do you need to change according to this chapter?

4. What habits do you need to develop according to this chapter?

Week 15; Day 2—Date _____
I Thessalonians 1-2

(In the space below, write any notes or thoughts you have regarding the text you are reading today.)

Thought Questions:

1. Write briefly what you have learned from this chapter?

2. Where do you fall short according to this chapter?

3. What do you need to change according to this chapter?

4. What habits do you need to develop according to this chapter?

Questions regarding today's reading:

1. Who wrote this letter?

2. Where had the word of the Lord sounded for from Thessalonica?

3. How had Paul, Silvanus and Timothy proven themselves to behave among the Thessalonians?

4. How did the Thessalonians accept the word from Paul?

5. Why had Paul not been able to come to Thessalonica again?

Week 15; Day 3—Date _____
I Thessalonians 3-4

(In the space below, write any notes or thoughts you have regarding the text you are reading today.)

Questions regarding today's reading:

1. Why did Paul send Timothy to Thessalonica?

2. In what did Paul pray that the Lord would cause the Thessalonians to increase and abound?

3. For what purpose has God called us?

4. What did Paul want the Thessalonians to make their ambition?

5. Who will rise first?

Thought Questions:

1. Write briefly what you have learned from this chapter?

2. Where do you fall short according to this chapter?

3. What do you need to change according to this chapter?

4. What habits do you need to develop according to this chapter?

Week 15; Day 4—Date _____
I Thessalonians 5-II Thessalonians 1
(In the space below, write any notes or thoughts you have regarding the text you are reading today.)

Questions regarding today's reading:
1. How will the day of the Lord come?

2. Who were the Thessalonians to appreciate and honor?

3. To what should we hold fast and from what should we abstain?

4. Who will God repay with affliction?

5. To what end did Paul always pray for the Thessalonians?

Thought Questions:
1. Write briefly what you have learned from this chapter?

2. Where do you fall short according to this chapter?

3. What do you need to change according to this chapter?

4. What habits do you need to develop according to this chapter?

Week 15; Day 5—Date _____
II Thessalonians 2-3

(In the space below, write any notes or thoughts you have regarding the text you are reading today.)

Questions regarding today's reading:

1. What must come before the day of the Lord?

2. Through what had God given the Thessalonians salvation?

3. For what did Paul what the Thessalonians to pray?

4. From whom were the Thessalonians to keep away?

5. Of what were the Thessalonians not to grow weary?

Thought Questions:

1. Write briefly what you have learned from this chapter?

2. Where do you fall short according to this chapter?

3. What do you need to change according to this chapter?

4. What habits do you need to develop according to this chapter?

Week 15—Group Discussion
II Corinthians 12–II Thessalonians 3

1. What were the most important lessons you learned from this week's readings?

2. Which lessons from this week's readings had the most profound practical impact on your daily life?

3. What questions do you have about this week's readings?

4. What lessons from this week's readings do you need any help with?

5. In **II Corinthians 12:1-2**, Paul said he had been given a thorn in the flesh. On the one hand, it appears to be from God to keep him humble. On the other hand, he says it was a messenger of Satan. Considering this, how does God use even the negative things in our lives (the things that even come from Satan) to help us grow in Christ?

6. In **I Thessalonians 4**, Paul talked about the standards of morality and purity we ought to have. Describe those standards and how we can maintain those standards in our immoral world?

7. In the letters to the Thessalonians, Paul says quite a bit about the work ethic Christians should have. Describe that ethic and give advice for maintaining such a work ethic in the modern world of laziness and apathy?

8. In **II Thessalonians 3:13**, Paul warned the Thessalonians not to grow weary of doing good. What might cause us to grow weary of doing good? What advice would you give to help us overcome that?

Week 16; Day 1—Date _____
Matthew 1-2

(In the space below, write any notes or thoughts you have regarding the text you are reading today.)

Thought Questions:

1. Write briefly what you have learned from this chapter?

2. Where do you fall short according to this chapter?

3. What do you need to change according to this chapter?

Questions regarding today's reading:

1. Of whom was Mary found to be with child?

2. What does "Immanuel" mean?

3. What did the magi or wise men give the child Jesus?

4. What habits do you need to develop according to this chapter?

4. Where did God tell Joseph to take the child Jesus?

5. In which city did Joseph, Mary and Jesus end up living?

Week 16; Day 2—Date _____
Matthew 3-4
(In the space below, write any notes or thoughts you have regarding the text you are reading today.)

Thought Questions:

1. Write briefly what you have learned from this chapter?

2. Where do you fall short according to this chapter?

3. What do you need to change according to this chapter?

4. What habits do you need to develop according to this chapter?

Questions regarding today's reading:

1. What did Isaiah prophecy that was about John the Baptist?

2. For what reason did Jesus ask John to baptize him?

3. What did the devil promise Jesus if He would worship the devil?

4. Where is Capernaum?

5. What did Jesus go throughout all Galilee proclaiming?

Week 16; Day 3—Date _____
Matthew 5-6

(In the space below, write any notes or thoughts you have regarding the text you are reading today.)

1. Write briefly what you have learned from this chapter?

2. Where do you fall short according to this chapter?

3. What do you need to change according to this chapter?

Questions regarding today's reading:

1. What belongs to the poor in spirit?

2. Whose righteousness must we surpass if we want to enter the kingdom of heaven?

3. For whom are we to pray?

4. What habits do you need to develop according to this chapter?

4. What happens to treasures stored up on earth?

5. What are we to seek first?

Week 16; Day 4—Date _____
Matthew 7-8
(In the space below, write any notes or thoughts you have regarding the text you are reading today.)

_____

Questions regarding today's reading:

1. How should we treat others?

2. Why were the crowds amazed at Jesus' teaching?

3. What did Jesus tell the healed leper to do?

4. Where did the Son of Man have to lay His head?

5. What did the people of the Gadarenes ask Jesus to do after He cleansed the demon-possessed men?

Thought Questions:

1. Write briefly what you have learned from this chapter?

2. Where do you fall short according to this chapter?

3. What do you need to change according to this chapter?

4. What habits do you need to develop according to this chapter?

Week 16; Day 5—Date _____
Matthew 9-10

(In the space below, write any notes or thoughts you have regarding the text you are reading today.)

Questions regarding today's reading:

1. Who did Jesus come to the earth to call?

2. What did the two blind men cry out as Jesus passed by them?

3. What were the disciples to ask of the Lord of Harvest?

4. When Jesus sent out the twelve, what did He tell them to proclaim?

5. What did Jesus come to the earth to bring?

Thought Questions:

1. Write briefly what you have learned from this chapter?

2. Where do you fall short according to this chapter?

3. What do you need to change according to this chapter?

4. What habits do you need to develop according to this chapter?

Week 16—Group Discussion
Matthew 1-10

1. What were the most important lessons you learned from this week's readings?

2. Which lessons from this week's readings had the most profound practical impact on your daily life?

3. What questions do you have about this week's readings?

4. What lessons from this week's readings do you need any help with?

5. In **Matthew 4**, we see Jesus overcome temptation. What lessons do you learn about dealing with temptation from that passage? What other advice for overcoming temptation and sin would you give other Christians?

6. **Matthew 5:3-12** is one of the richest passages in the entire Bible describing how the kingdom citizen ought to live. What did you learn from these verses about being a faithful citizen of God's kingdom?

7. How can we mirror our prayer lives after the prayer lessons Jesus taught in the Sermon on the Mount?

8. How can we be an answer to the prayer found in **Matthew 9:36-38** today?

Week 17; Day 1—Date _____
Matthew 11-12

(In the space below, write any notes or thoughts you have regarding the text you are reading today.)

1. Write briefly what you have learned from this chapter?

2. Where do you fall short according to this chapter?

3. What do you need to change according to this chapter?

Questions regarding today's reading:

1. What question did John the Baptist have for Jesus?

2. Why did Jesus denounce and rebuke the cities where He performed His miracles?

3. Why did those in the synagogue question Jesus regarding healing on the Sabbath?

4. By whom did the Pharisees claim Jesus cast out demons?

5. Who did Jesus say were His mother and brothers?

4. What habits do you need to develop according to this chapter?

Week 17; Day 2—Date _____
Matthew 13-14

(In the space below, write any notes or thoughts you have regarding the text you are reading today.)

1. Write briefly what you have learned from this chapter?

2. Where do you fall short according to this chapter?

3. What do you need to change according to this chapter?

_____

Questions regarding today's reading:

1. What were the four soils in Jesus' parable?

2. What is the kingdom of heaven like according to Jesus' parables?

3. Where is a prophet not accepted?

4. Why had Herod imprisoned John the Baptist?

4. What habits do you need to develop according to this chapter?

5. According to Jesus, why did Peter sink in the water?

Week 17; Day 3—Date _____
Matthew 15-16

(In the space below, write any notes or thoughts you have regarding the text you are reading today.)

Thought Questions:

1. Write briefly what you have learned from this chapter?

2. Where do you fall short according to this chapter?

3. What do you need to change according to this chapter?

Questions regarding today's reading:

1. What did Jesus say Isaiah had said about the ones who questioned Him?

2. What did Jesus say about the Canaanite woman's faith?

3. Of what did Jesus tell His disciples to beware?

4. What habits do you need to develop according to this chapter?

4. Who did the disciples believe Jesus to be?

5. What must Jesus' disciple take up if we wish to follow Him?

Week 17; Day 4—Date _____
Matthew 17-18
(In the space below, write any notes or thoughts you have regarding the text you are reading today.)

_____

Questions regarding today's reading:

1. Who stood with Jesus on the Mount of Transfiguration?

2. What did the voice from heaven say about Jesus?

3. Who is the greatest in the kingdom of heaven?

4. How often did Jesus say we should forgive our brother?

5. From where must we forgive our brother?

Thought Questions:

1. Write briefly what you have learned from this chapter?

2. Where do you fall short according to this chapter?

3. What do you need to change according to this chapter?

4. What habits do you need to develop according to this chapter?

Week 17; Day 5—Date _____
Matthew 19-20
(In the space below, write any notes or thoughts you have regarding the text you are reading today.)

Thought Questions:
1. Write briefly what you have learned from this chapter?

2. Where do you fall short according to this chapter?

3. What do you need to change according to this chapter?

4. What habits do you need to develop according to this chapter?

Questions regarding today's reading:

1. What did Jesus call it if a man divorces his wife for any reason other than immorality and then marries another woman?

2. To whom does the kingdom of heaven belong?

3. What did Jesus say would happen to Him in Jerusalem?

4. What request did the mother of the sons of Zebedee make?

5. What must we become if we wish to be great among Christ's disciples?

Week 17—Group Discussion
Matthew 11-20

1. What were the most important lessons you learned from this week's readings?

2. Which lessons from this week's readings had the most profound practical impact on your daily life?

3. What questions do you have about this week's readings?

4. What lessons from this week's readings do you need any help with?

5. We often have a tendency to wish we could perform miracles to convince others of the truth. According to **Matthew 11:20**, how much benefit would miraculous gifts really be for this purpose?

6. How is Jesus' yoke easy and light?

7. How do Isaiah's words, quoted in **Matthew 15:8-9**, apply to people today as well?

8. How do we sometimes follow in Peter's footsteps in **Matthew 16:23**?

9. What do you think Jesus meant when He said the kingdom of heaven belonged to such as the little children?

Week 18; Day 1—Date _____
Matthew 21-22

(In the space below, write any notes or thoughts you have regarding the text you are reading today.)

Thought Questions:

1. Write briefly what you have learned from this chapter?

2. Where do you fall short according to this chapter?

3. What do you need to change according to this chapter?

4. What habits do you need to develop according to this chapter?

Questions regarding today's reading:

1. What did the crowds do as Jesus entered Jerusalem?

2. Who did Jesus say would enter the kingdom of God ahead of the chief priests and elders of the people?

3. With whom did the Pharisees conspire to question Jesus about taxes?

4. Whose wife did Jesus claim the woman in the Saducees' story would be?

5. On which two commandments do the Law and Prophets rest?

Week 18; Day 2—Date _____
Matthew 23-24

(In the space below, write any notes or thoughts you have regarding the text you are reading today.)

1. Write briefly what you have learned from this chapter?

2. Where do you fall short according to this chapter?

3. What do you need to change according to this chapter?

_____

Questions regarding today's reading:

1. In whose chair did the scribes and the Pharisees seat themselves?

2. What did Jesus say the Jews would do with the prophets God sent them?

3. According to Jesus, why was He unable to gather Jerusalem under His protective wings?

4. What habits do you need to develop according to this chapter?

4. What was going to happen to Jerusalem's buildings?

5. What will the master do for the faithful and sensible servant?

Week 18; Day 3—Date _____
Matthew 25-26

(In the space below, write any notes or thoughts you have regarding the text you are reading today.)

1. Write briefly what you have learned from this chapter?

2. Where do you fall short according to this chapter?

3. What do you need to change according to this chapter?

4. What habits do you need to develop according to this chapter?

_____

Questions regarding today's reading:

1. How did the prudent virgins behave more wisely than the others?

2. What did the one-talent man do with his money?

3. What were the priests willing to give Judas to betray Jesus?

4. Who did Jesus take deeper into the garden on the night of His betrayal?

5. To whom did those who seized Jesus first take Him?

Week 18; Day 4—Date _____
Matthew 27-28

(In the space below, write any notes or thoughts you have regarding the text you are reading today.)

1. Write briefly what you have learned from this chapter?

2. Where do you fall short according to this chapter?

3. What do you need to change according to this chapter?

Questions regarding today's reading:

1. What sin did Judas claim he committed?

2. What was written above Jesus' head on the cross?

3. Who took the body of Jesus in order to bury it?

4. Where the disciples supposed to go in order to see Jesus?

5. How much authority did Jesus claim had been given to Him?

4. What habits do you need to develop according to this chapter?

Week 18; Day 5—Date _____
Hebrews 1-2

(In the space below, write any notes or thoughts you have regarding the text you are reading today.)

Thought Questions:

1. Write briefly what you have learned from this chapter?

2. Where do you fall short according to this chapter?

3. What do you need to change according to this chapter?

4. What habits do you need to develop according to this chapter?

Questions regarding today's reading:

1. Through whom has God spoken to us in these last days?

2. What kind of spirits are angels?

3. How did God testify to the word of salvation?

4. For whom did Jesus taste death?

5. Why is Jesus able to come to the aid of the tempted?

Week 18—Group Discussion
Matthew 21-Hebrews 2

1. What were the most important lessons you learned from this week's readings?

2. Which lessons from this week's readings had the most profound practical impact on your daily life?

3. What questions do you have about this week's readings?

4. What lessons from this week's readings do you need any help with?

5. How can we grow to be one of God's greatest children according to **Matthew 23:11**? How do we accomplish this on a practical level?

6. How do the parables of judgment in **Matthew 24:42-25:46** apply to us?

7. Based on the parable from **Matthew 25:31-46**, how do we serve Jesus?

8. According to **Hebrews 2**, what has Jesus done for us through His suffering and death?

9. How does Jesus help us in our temptations today?

Week 19; Day 1—Date _____
Hebrews 3-4

(In the space below, write any notes or thoughts you have regarding the text you are reading today.)

1. Write briefly what you have learned from this chapter?

2. Where do you fall short according to this chapter?

3. What do you need to change according to this chapter?

Questions regarding today's reading:

1. Who is the Apostle and High Priest of our confession?

2. Why were the Israelites unable to enter the Promised Land?

3. Why did the word that the Israelites heard not profit them?

4. What kind of rest remains for the people of God?

5. Why should we draw near the throne of grace?

4. What habits do you need to develop according to this chapter?

Week 19; Day 2—Date _____
Hebrews 5-6
(In the space below, write any notes or thoughts you have regarding the text you are reading today.)

_____

Questions regarding today's reading:

1. What did Jesus offer up in the days of His flesh?

2. According to what order is Jesus a high priest?

3. Who is solid food for?

4. By whom did God swear when He made an oath to Abraham?

5. What is it impossible for God to do?

Thought Questions:

1. Write briefly what you have learned from this chapter?

2. Where do you fall short according to this chapter?

3. What do you need to change according to this chapter?

4. What habits do you need to develop according to this chapter?

Week 19; Day 3—Date _____
Hebrews 7-8

(In the space below, write any notes or thoughts you have regarding the text you are reading today.)

Thought Questions:

1. Write briefly what you have learned from this chapter?

2. Where do you fall short according to this chapter?

3. What do you need to change according to this chapter?

4. What habits do you need to develop according to this chapter?

Questions regarding today's reading:

1. Of what was Melchizedek king? Of whom was he the priest?

2. When the priesthood changes, what else also changes?

3. Why does Jesus hold His priesthood forever?

4. How has Jesus obtained a more excellent ministry than the Old Testament priests?

5. When God established the New Covenant, what happened to the Old?

Week 19; Day 4—Date _____

Hebrews 9-10

(In the space below, write any notes or thoughts you have regarding the text you are reading today.)

_____

Questions regarding today's reading:

1. Who was able to enter the Holy of Holies under the Old Law and how often did they enter?

2. Through whose blood did Jesus enter the more perfect tabernacle?

3. What comes after men die?

4. Where did Jesus sit after offering His sacrifice for sins?

5. What will we receive when we have endured, doing the will of God?

Thought Questions:

1. Write briefly what you have learned from this chapter?

2. Where do you fall short according to this chapter?

3. What do you need to change according to this chapter?

4. What habits do you need to develop according to this chapter?

Week 19; Day 5—Date _____
Hebrews 11-12

(In the space below, write any notes or thoughts you have regarding the text you are reading today.)

1. Write briefly what you have learned from this chapter?

2. Where do you fall short according to this chapter?

3. What do you need to change according to this chapter?

4. What habits do you need to develop according to this chapter?

Questions regarding today's reading:

1. What is faith?

2. What did Joseph mention by faith as he was dying?

3. How should we run the race set before us?

4. What fruit does discipline yield in those trained by it?

5. What kind of kingdom do we receive?

Week 19—Group Discussion
Hebrews 3-12

1. What were the most important lessons you learned from this week's readings?

2. Which lessons from this week's readings had the most profound practical impact on your daily life?

3. What questions do you have about this week's readings?

4. What lessons from this week's readings do you need any help with?

5. According to **Hebrews 3:6**, we are Christ's house if we hold fast until the end. Based on this week's reading, what forces work against our holding fast and what can we do to strengthen our hold?

6. What did you learn about growth in Christ from **Hebrews 5:11-6:8**?

7. What does it mean to stimulate one another to love and good deeds? How do we do that?

8. How can we grow to have faith like the examples listed in **Hebrews 11**?

9. How does looking to the great cloud of witnesses, as advised in **Hebrews 12:1**, help us in our faith?

Week 20; Day 1—Date _____
Hebrews 13-James 1

(In the space below, write any notes or thoughts you have regarding the text you are reading today.)

1. Write briefly what you have learned from this chapter?

2. Where do you fall short according to this chapter?

3. What do you need to change according to this chapter?

Questions regarding today's reading:

1. What must we allow to continue?

2. What are we to offer up to God through Jesus Christ?

3. How are we to consider it when we encounter trials?

4. What habits do you need to develop according to this chapter?

4. What has the Lord promised to those who love Him?

5. What is pure and undefiled religion?

Week 20; Day 2—Date _____

James 2-3

(In the space below, write any notes or thoughts you have regarding the text you are reading today.)

Thought Questions:

1. Write briefly what you have learned from this chapter?

2. Where do you fall short according to this chapter?

3. What do you need to change according to this chapter?

4. What habits do you need to develop according to this chapter?

Questions regarding today's reading:

1. What are we doing if we show partiality among brethren?

2. What is faith if it doesn't have any works?

3. By what is a man justified?

4. What small part of our body can cause us big problems?

5. How can we demonstrate our wisdom?

Week 20; Day 3—Date _____
James 4-5
(In the space below, write any notes or thoughts you have regarding the text you are reading today.)

_____

Questions regarding today's reading:

1. What is the source of quarrels?

2. What is it if we know the right thing to do, but do not do it?

3. For what are the brethren to be patient?

4. What should we do if we are suffering? ...cheerful?

5. From what do we save a sinner if we turn him from the error of his way?

Thought Questions:

1. Write briefly what you have learned from this chapter?

2. Where do you fall short according to this chapter?

3. What do you need to change according to this chapter?

4. What habits do you need to develop according to this chapter?

Week 20; Day 4—Date _____
Philemon-I Timothy 1
(In the space below, write any notes or thoughts you have regarding the text you are reading today.)

Thought Questions:
1. Write briefly what you have learned from this chapter?

2. Where do you fall short according to this chapter?

3. What do you need to change according to this chapter?

4. What habits do you need to develop according to this chapter?

_____

Questions regarding today's reading:

1. For whom was Paul appealing to Philemon?

2. What did Paul know Philemon would do?

3. What did Paul urge Timothy to instruct certain men?

4. What had Paul formerly been?

5. Why had Paul delivered Hymenaeus and Alexander over to Satan?

Week 20; Day 5—Date _____
I Timothy 2-3

(In the space below, write any notes or thoughts you have regarding the text you are reading today.)

Questions regarding today's reading:

1. For whom should prayers be made?

2. Who was first created?

3. What must an overseer (bishop) be?

4. What must deacons be?

5. What is the household of God?

Thought Questions:

1. Write briefly what you have learned from this chapter?

2. Where do you fall short according to this chapter?

3. What do you need to change according to this chapter?

4. What habits do you need to develop according to this chapter?

1. What were the most important lessons you learned from this week's readings?

2. Which lessons from this week's readings had the most profound practical impact on your daily life?

3. What questions do you have about this week's readings?

4. What lessons from this week's readings do you need any help with?

5. **Hebrews 13:1** says to let love of the brethren continue. Within the context of that passage, how do we demonstrate love to brethren? What obstacles do you believe keep us from this kind of love and how can we overcome them?

6. Why should we obey our leaders in Christ's church?

7. How can we maintain joy even throughout trials as **James 1:2** teaches?

8. What advice would you give to help others learn to control their tongues, which **James 3** says is a small organ which causes great trouble?

9. What do you think Paul meant when he wrote that the goal of our instruction is love in **I Timothy 1:5**?

Week 21; Day 1—Date _____
I Timothy 4-5

(In the space below, write any notes or thoughts you have regarding the text you are reading today.)

1. Write briefly what you have learned from this chapter?

2. Where do you fall short according to this chapter?

3. What do you need to change according to this chapter?

4. What habits do you need to develop according to this chapter?

Questions regarding today's reading:

1. How is our food sanctified?

2. What is profitable for all things?

3. In what should we be good examples?

4. How did Paul describe those who would not provide for their own families?

5. From what was Timothy to keep himself free?

Week 21; Day 2—Date _____
I Timothy 6-II Timothy 1
(In the space below, write any notes or thoughts you have regarding the text you are reading today.)

1. Write briefly what you have learned from this chapter?

2. Where do you fall short according to this chapter?

3. What do you need to change according to this chapter?

4. What habits do you need to develop according to this chapter?

Questions regarding today's reading:

1. When is godliness a means of great gain?

2. What is the root of all sorts of evil?

3. Upon whom must we fix our hope?

4. From whom did Timothy learn to have a sincere faith?

5. What standard did Paul encourage Timothy to maintain?

Week 21; Day 3—Date _____
II Timothy 2-3

(In the space below, write any notes or thoughts you have regarding the text you are reading today.)

Thought Questions:

1. Write briefly what you have learned from this chapter?

2. Where do you fall short according to this chapter?

3. What do you need to change according to this chapter?

Questions regarding today's reading:

1. What was Timothy to entrust to faithful men?

2. As what must we be diligent to present ourselves?

3. What must the Lord's bond-servant be?

4. What will happen to all who desire to live godly in Christ Jesus?

5. For what is Scripture profitable?

4. What habits do you need to develop according to this chapter?

II Timothy 4-Titus 1

(In the space below, write any notes or thoughts you have regarding the text you are reading today.)

Thought Questions:

1. Write briefly what you have learned from this chapter?

2. Where do you fall short according to this chapter?

3. What do you need to change according to this chapter?

_____

Questions regarding today's reading:

1. What did Paul exhort Timothy to preach?

2. What was Timothy to bring to Paul when he went to him?

3. For what reason had Paul left Titus in Crete?

4. Why must rebellious men and empty talkers be silence?

5. How do these men deny God?

4. What habits do you need to develop according to this chapter?

Week 21; Day 5—Date _____
Titus 2-3
(In the space below, write any notes or thoughts you have regarding the text you are reading today.)

Questions regarding today's reading:

1. What things did Paul tell Titus to speak?

2. What has the grace of God instructed us to do?

3. According to what did God save us?

4. What must those who trust God avoid?

5. In what must Christians learn to engage?

Thought Questions:

1. Write briefly what you have learned from this chapter?

2. Where do you fall short according to this chapter?

3. What do you need to change according to this chapter?

4. What habits do you need to develop according to this chapter?

1. What were the most important lessons you learned from this week's readings?

2. Which lessons from this week's readings had the most profound practical impact on your daily life?

3. What questions do you have about this week's readings?

4. What lessons from this week's readings do you need any help with?

5. How can we demonstrate the proper example as explained by Paul in **I Timothy 4:12** and **Titus 2:7-8**?

6. What did you learn about how we should relate to money from **I Timothy 6**?

7. How can we be vessels for honor as described in **II Timothy 2**?

8. What does **II Timothy 3:12** mean about our lives as Christians?

9. Based on **II Timothy 3:16-17**, how should we use the Scriptures?

Week 22; Day 1—Date _____

John 1-2

(In the space below, write any notes or thoughts you have regarding the text you are reading today.)

Thought Questions:

1. Write briefly what you have learned from this chapter?

2. Where do you fall short according to this chapter?

3. What do you need to change according to this chapter?

4. What habits do you need to develop according to this chapter?

Questions regarding today's reading:

1. Who was the witness sent to testify of the Light?

2. What did John claim he was when questioned by the Levites and priests?

3. What did John claim Jesus was?

4. What was the beginning of Jesus' signs in Cana of Galilee?

5. When Jesus said, "Destroy this temple, and in three days I will raise it up," of what was He actually speaking?

Week 22; Day 2—Date _____
John 3-4
(In the space below, write any notes or thoughts you have regarding the text you are reading today.)

Questions regarding today's reading:
1. Of what must a person be born to enter the kingdom of God?

2. Why did God send the Son into the world?

3. At whose well was Jesus resting in Samaria?

4. How will the true worshipers worship God?

5. When did the fever leave the royal official's son?

Week 22; Day 3—Date _____
John 5-6
(In the space below, write any notes or thoughts you have regarding the text you are reading today.)

1. Write briefly what you have learned from this chapter?

2. Where do you fall short according to this chapter?

3. What do you need to change according to this chapter?

Questions regarding today's reading:
1. What was the name of the pool where the lame and sick would wait?

2. What did Jesus say testified regarding who He was?

3. With what did Jesus feed the large crowd that followed Him?

4. What habits do you need to develop according to this chapter?

4. What did Jesus claim was the bread of life?

5. Why did Peter say the twelve would not abandon Jesus?

Week 22; Day 4—Date _____
John 7-8

(In the space below, write any notes or thoughts you have regarding the text you are reading today.)

_____

Questions regarding today's reading:

1. For what reason did Jesus claim the world hated Him?

2. How are we supposed to judge?

3. Who did Jesus claim should cast the first stone at the woman caught in adultery?

4. Who did Jesus always please?

5. What did Jesus say He was before Abraham was born?

Thought Questions:

1. Write briefly what you have learned from this chapter?

2. Where do you fall short according to this chapter?

3. What do you need to change according to this chapter?

4. What habits do you need to develop according to this chapter?

Week 22; Day 5—Date _____
John 9-10

(In the space below, write any notes or thoughts you have regarding the text you are reading today.)

_____

Questions regarding today's reading:

1. Why had the man been born blind according to Jesus?

2. Of whom did the Pharisees claim to be disciples?

3. Who is the door of the sheep?

4. How many flocks would Jesus have and how many shepherds would there be?

5. For what reason did the Jews claim they were going to stone Jesus?

Thought Questions:

1. Write briefly what you have learned from this chapter?

2. Where do you fall short according to this chapter?

3. What do you need to change according to this chapter?

4. What habits do you need to develop according to this chapter?

Week 22—Group Discussion
John 1-10

1. What were the most important lessons you learned from this week's readings?

2. Which lessons from this week's readings had the most profound practical impact on your daily life?

3. What questions do you have about this week's readings?

4. What lessons from this week's readings do you need any help with?

5. What great example did Andrew and Philip set regarding personal evangelism in **John 1** and how can we follow it?

6. What do you think it means to worship God in spirit and truth?

7. How do we follow Jesus' example in **John 4:34** and make God's will our food?

8. What does it mean to work for the food which endures to eternal life?

9. Why is it comforting to know that Jesus is our Good Shepherd?

Week 23; Day 1—Date _____
John 11-12
(In the space below, write any notes or thoughts you have regarding the text you are reading today.)

_____

Questions regarding today's reading:

1. For what purpose did Jesus claim Lazarus had become sick?

2. What did Thomas say to encourage the disciples to follow Jesus into Judea?

3. What did Caiaphas say in response to Jesus' miracle?

4. What did the priests plan to do with Lazarus?

5. What did Jesus claim would judge the unbeliever?

Thought Questions:

1. Write briefly what you have learned from this chapter?

2. Where do you fall short according to this chapter?

3. What do you need to change according to this chapter?

4. What habits do you need to develop according to this chapter?

Week 23; Day 2—Date _____
John 13-14

(In the space below, write any notes or thoughts you have regarding the text you are reading today.)

1. Write briefly what you have learned from this chapter?

2. Where do you fall short according to this chapter?

3. What do you need to change according to this chapter?

Questions regarding today's reading:

1. What service did Jesus give His disciples during His last Passover with them?

2. What was the new commandment Jesus gave His disciples?

3. How did Jesus claim people must get to the Father?

4. What habits do you need to develop according to this chapter?

4. Who would the Father send when Jesus was gone?

5. How can the world know that Jesus loved the Father?

Week 23; Day 3—Date _____
John 15-16
(In the space below, write any notes or thoughts you have regarding the text you are reading today.)

1. Write briefly what you have learned from this chapter?

2. Where do you fall short according to this chapter?

3. What do you need to change according to this chapter?

Questions regarding today's reading:

1. When can we bear fruit?

2. What is the greatest love one man can demonstrate to another?

3. Why was it to the disciples' advantage for Christ to leave?

4. Into what would the Spirit guide the apostles?

5. Why were the disciples to take courage?

4. What habits do you need to develop according to this chapter?

Week 23; Day 4—Date _____
John 17-18

(In the space below, write any notes or thoughts you have regarding the text you are reading today.)

_____

Questions regarding today's reading:

1. Why did Jesus want to be glorified?

2. What was Jesus' prayer for all His disciples of all time?

3. What did Peter do to Malchus?

4. How did Jesus respond when struck by one of the officers?

5. What did Jesus claim about His kingdom to Pilate?

Thought Questions:

1. Write briefly what you have learned from this chapter?

2. Where do you fall short according to this chapter?

3. What do you need to change according to this chapter?

4. What habits do you need to develop according to this chapter?

Week 23; Day 5—Date _____
John 19-20

(In the space below, write any notes or thoughts you have regarding the text you are reading today.)

2. Where do you fall short according to this chapter?

3. What do you need to change according to this chapter?

Questions regarding today's reading:

1. Why did Pilate bring Jesus out to the Jews again?

2. How did the soldiers determine who would get Jesus' tunic?

3. Who requested to take and bury the body of Jesus?

4. What did Jesus tell Mary Magdalene to tell the disciples?

5. Why were the signs recorded in this book?

4. What habits do you need to develop according to this chapter?

Week 23—Group Discussion
John 11-20

1. What were the most important lessons you learned from this week's readings?

2. Which lessons from this week's readings had the most profound practical impact on your daily life?

3. What questions do you have about this week's readings?

4. What lessons from this week's readings do you need any help with?

5. What does it mean to love God and to love Jesus?

6. According to **John 15**, how do we prove ourselves to be Jesus' disciples? How do we accomplish this?

7. Why did the world hate Jesus? Why will it hate us?

8. What does the crucifixion mean to you?

9. What does the resurrection mean to you?

Week 24; Day 1—Date _____
John 21-I John 1

(In the space below, write any notes or thoughts you have regarding the text you are reading today.)

1. Write briefly what you have learned from this chapter?

2. Where do you fall short according to this chapter?

3. What do you need to change according to this chapter?

Questions regarding today's reading:

1. What did Peter and the other disciples decide to do while waiting near the Sea of Tiberius?

2. What did Jesus ask Simon Peter three times?

3. How many other signs and deeds did Jesus accomplish?

4. Why did John write **I John**?

5. What is God faithful to do if we confess our sins?

4. What habits do you need to develop according to this chapter?

Week 24; Day 2—Date _____
I John 2-3
(In the space below, write any notes or thoughts you have regarding the text you are reading today.)

Thought Questions:

1. Write briefly what you have learned from this chapter?

2. Where do you fall short according to this chapter?

3. What do you need to change according to this chapter?

4. What habits do you need to develop according to this chapter?

Questions regarding today's reading:

1. How do we know that we have come to know Jesus?

2. How did John describe the things of the world?

3. Who is antichrist?

4. What will we be when Jesus appears?

5. How does John encourage us to love?

Week 24; Day 3—Date _____
I John 4-5

(In the space below, write any notes or thoughts you have regarding the text you are reading today.)

_____

Questions regarding today's reading:

1. How was the love of God manifested?

2. Why do we love?

3. How do we know that we love the children of God?

4. What has God given us through His Son?

5. From what does John encourage the brethren to guard themselves?

Thought Questions:

1. Write briefly what you have learned from this chapter?

2. Where do you fall short according to this chapter?

3. What do you need to change according to this chapter?

4. What habits do you need to develop according to this chapter?

Week 24; Day 4—Date _____
II John-III John
(In the space below, write any notes or thoughts you have regarding the text you are reading today.)

Questions regarding today's reading:

1. What did John initially ask of the "chosen lady"?

2. What did John say about those who do not abide in the doctrine of Christ?

3. According to **III John**, what made John very glad?

4. Who was wanting the preeminence among the brethren to whom John wrote?

5. Who had received a good testimony from everyone?

Thought Questions:

1. Write briefly what you have learned from this chapter?

2. Where do you fall short according to this chapter?

3. What do you need to change according to this chapter?

4. What habits do you need to develop according to this chapter?

Week 24; Day 5—Date _____
Revelation 1-2

(In the space below, write any notes or thoughts you have regarding the text you are reading today.)

1. Write briefly what you have learned from this chapter?

2. Where do you fall short according to this chapter?

3. What do you need to change according to this chapter?

Questions regarding today's reading:

1. When would the things take place that God was showing to His bond-servant John?

2. Of what was John a fellow partaker with the brethren?

3. What did Jesus have against the church at Ephesus?

4. What habits do you need to develop according to this chapter?

4. What will Jesus give to those who are faithful unto death?

5. What did Jesus know about the church in Thyatira?

Week 24—Group Discussion
John 21-Revelation 2

1. What were the most important lessons you learned from this week's readings?

2. Which lessons from this week's readings had the most profound practical impact on your daily life?

3. What questions do you have about this week's readings?

4. What lessons from this week's readings do you need any help with?

5. How does Jesus' conversation with Peter in **John 21** provide you comfort?

6. Look at John's description of the things of the world in **I John 2:15-17**. How do these things lead us into sin and how can we overcome them?

7. According to **I John**, how do we show ourselves to abide in God and show that Christ abides in us?

8. Why is the doctrine of Christ important according to **II John**?

9. How do we compare to the four churches we have read about so far in **Revelation**?

Week 25; Day 1—Date _____
Revelation 3-4
(In the space below, write any notes or thoughts you have regarding the text you are reading today.)

Questions regarding today's reading:

1. What would Jesus give to those of Sardis who would overcome?

2. Why would Jesus keep the church at Philadelphia from the hour of testing?

3. What did Jesus have against Laodicea?

4. What did John see sitting around the great throne in heaven?

5. What did the creatures and elders say about God?

Thought Questions:

1. Write briefly what you have learned from this chapter?

2. Where do you fall short according to this chapter?

3. What do you need to change according to this chapter?

4. What habits do you need to develop according to this chapter?

Week 25; Day 2—Date _____
Revelation 5-6
(In the space below, write any notes or thoughts you have regarding the text you are reading today.)

Thought Questions:

1. Write briefly what you have learned from this chapter?

2. Where do you fall short according to this chapter?

3. What do you need to change according to this chapter?

4. What habits do you need to develop according to this chapter?

Questions regarding today's reading:

1. Who was worthy to open the book and break its seals?

2. What did the elders and creatures say about the Lamb, the Lion of Judah?

3. What was given to the rider on the white horse?

4. What were the souls of the slain martyrs crying out from under the altar?

5. What happened when the Lamb broke the sixth seal?

Week 25; Day 3—Date _____
Revelation 7-8

(In the space below, write any notes or thoughts you have regarding the text you are reading today.)

Questions regarding today's reading:

1. For what did the angels have to wait before they could harm the earth or the sea?

2. How many people were around the throne of God clothed in white?

3. For how long was their silence in heaven when the seventh seal was broken?

4. What did the angel throw to the earth?

5. What did the eagle say as it flew through the heavens?

Thought Questions:

1. Write briefly what you have learned from this chapter?

2. Where do you fall short according to this chapter?

3. What do you need to change according to this chapter?

4. What habits do you need to develop according to this chapter?

Week 25; Day 4—Date _____
Revelation 9-10

(In the space below, write any notes or thoughts you have regarding the text you are reading today.)

_____

Questions regarding today's reading:

1. Which men were the locusts not to harm?

2. What did God say when the sixth trumpet was blown?

3. What does John tell us the people who were not slain in the judgment of the plagues and horsemen refrained from doing?

4. What was John not allowed to do regarding the seven thunders?

5. What did John do with the angel's little book?

Thought Questions:

1. Write briefly what you have learned from this chapter?

2. Where do you fall short according to this chapter?

3. What do you need to change according to this chapter?

4. What habits do you need to develop according to this chapter?

Week 25; Day 5—Date _____
Revelation 11-12

(In the space below, write any notes or thoughts you have regarding the text you are reading today.)

Questions regarding today's reading:

1. What happens to those who try to harm the two witnesses?

2. What happened to the witnesses 3 ½ days after their deaths?

3. Where was the temple of God at this time?

4. Why did the dragon stand before the woman?

5. Who was the dragon?

Thought Questions:

1. Write briefly what you have learned from this chapter?

2. Where do you fall short according to this chapter?

3. What do you need to change according to this chapter?

4. What habits do you need to develop according to this chapter?

1. What were the most important lessons you learned from this week's readings?

2. Which lessons from this week's readings had the most profound practical impact on your daily life?

3. What questions do you have about this week's readings?

4. What lessons from this week's readings do you need any help with?

5. How do we compare to the three churches we read about in **Revelation 3**?

6. Why are the Father and the Son so worthy?

7. Considering the first Christians who read **Revelation** were enduring tribulation (**cf. Revelation 1:9**), what significance do you think the martyred saints beneath the altar in **Revelation 6** had for them?

8. Why is the sealing of the bond-servants of God so important in this extremely graphic word picture?

9. According to **Revelation 12:11**, how did the brethren overcome the dragon?

Week 26; Day 1—Date _____
Revelation 13-14

(In the space below, write any notes or thoughts you have regarding the text you are reading today.)

1. Write briefly what you have learned from this chapter?

2. Where do you fall short according to this chapter?

3. What do you need to change according to this chapter?

4. What habits do you need to develop according to this chapter?

Questions regarding today's reading:

1. Who did the whole earth worship?

2. Who would not worship the beast and the dragon?

3. What did the earth beast give to all those who would worship the first beast and the dragon?

4. What did the three angels say as they flew?

5. Why are the dead who die in the Lord blessed?

Week 26; Day 2—Date _____
Revelation 15-16

(In the space below, write any notes or thoughts you have regarding the text you are reading today.)

_____

Questions regarding today's reading:

1. Who sang the song of Moses?

2. What did the living creature give to the seven angels?

3. For what reason did God have the bowls of wrath poured out according to the third angel?

4. How did the kingdom of the beast respond to the judgments of God?

5. What did the voice from heaven say when the seventh bowl was poured out?

Thought Questions:

1. Write briefly what you have learned from this chapter?

2. Where do you fall short according to this chapter?

3. What do you need to change according to this chapter?

4. What habits do you need to develop according to this chapter?

Week 26; Day 3—Date _____
Revelation 17-18

(In the space below, write any notes or thoughts you have regarding the text you are reading today.)

Questions regarding today's reading:

1. What was written on the forehead of the woman clothed in purple?

2. What did the angel say the woman really was?

3. What did a different angel cry out about Babylon the great?

4. Why would the kings of the earth mourn and lament?

5. Whose blood was found in Babylon the great?

Thought Questions:

1. Write briefly what you have learned from this chapter?

2. Where do you fall short according to this chapter?

3. What do you need to change according to this chapter?

4. What habits do you need to develop according to this chapter?

Week 26; Day 4—Date _____
Revelation 19-20
(In the space below, write any notes or thoughts you have regarding the text you are reading today.)

Questions regarding today's reading:

1. Why does glory and power belong to God according to the heavenly multitude?

2. Why was John not allowed to worship the angel of the Lord?

3. What happened to the beast and the false prophet?

4. For how long would the martyrs reign with Jesus?

5. What ultimately happened to the devil?

Thought Questions:

1. Write briefly what you have learned from this chapter?

2. Where do you fall short according to this chapter?

3. What do you need to change according to this chapter?

4. What habits do you need to develop according to this chapter?

Week 26; Day 5—Date _____
Revelation 21-22

(In the space below, write any notes or thoughts you have regarding the text you are reading today.)

Questions regarding today's reading:

1. What was John being shown as he looked at the "new" Jerusalem?

2. Why was there no temple in the heavenly city?

3. When would the things in this book take place?

4. What does Jesus claim to be?

5. What happens to those who change the words of this prophetic book?

Thought Questions:

1. Write briefly what you have learned from this chapter?

2. Where do you fall short according to this chapter?

3. What do you need to change according to this chapter?

4. What habits do you need to develop according to this chapter?

1. What were the most important lessons you learned from this week's readings?

2. Which lessons from this week's readings had the most profound practical impact on your daily life?

3. What questions do you have about this week's readings?

4. What lessons from this week's readings do you need any help with?

5. Contrast the time the devil is able to allow his kings to reign in **Revelation 17:12** with the time the martyrs reign with Jesus in **Revelation 20:4**?

6. In **Revelation**, what ultimately happens to all who oppose God? …to all who persevere in serving the Lord?

7. Considering the above, what do you believe **Revelation** is really all about?

8. **Revelation 22:18-19** contains powerful warnings against altering God's word. Based on these verses, why do you think it is important to continue studying God's word?

9. What have you gained from reading through the New Testament over the last six months?